A BRILL[IANT LIGHT OPENED] UP IN FRO[NT...]

He was in the passenger's seat, dozing, when the driver hit a patch of black ice, the car swerved, and they slammed into a tree . . .

"There was no pain . . . I know the color was generally gray around me . . .

"I had a sense that time was passing . . ."

There was nothing else . . . until a brilliant light opened up in front of him. . . .

"It was just there. I didn't move toward it. It didn't move toward me. It was just like someone had switched a light on right in front of me. It was a brilliant light, more like a sheet of light than a single point . . ."

Suddenly, he was aware of a voice that seemed to be coming from the light.

"I didn't hear anyone speak exactly, but I knew that someone was communicating with me very clearly and directly. I tried to see a face but I couldn't."

. . . "Before this happened I was just—I had these millions of questions to ask and in an instant they were all literally answered . . ."

And then he woke up in the wrecked car, soaked in gasoline and aware that the ignition to the engine was on. The engine had stopped but the lights were still burning. He was bleeding from his injuries and his friend, the driver, was still unconscious.

Although he knew he was badly hurt, and aware of the gasoline around him, he still had this feeling of great inner peace. He'd been told that everything was going to be fine. It would be all right.

TO TOUCH THE LIGHT

KEVIN D. RANDLE

PINNACLE BOOKS
WINDSOR PUBLISHING CORP.

TABLE OF CONTENTS

Introduction

Like many Americans, I have always wondered about—and been a little frightened by—the concept of death. It is the great unknown, and the unknown is always frightening. To answer our questions about it, we have looked to religion, and sometimes to science, but the answers found there have always been less than satisfactory.

Death is a part of life. Family, friends, lovers . . . everyone grows older and all eventually die. It is hard to watch the terminally ill waste away and then slip away. But we don't talk about it because it is something that we can always discuss tomorrow or the next day or next week. After all, we have forever.

And that might be the key. Maybe we do have forever. Edgar Cayce, among others, tells us that we are all born again and again, as we strive to obtain a state of perfection. Death is merely a transition from one state of existence into another—not unlike birth, which moves us from a world of all warmth and darkness into one that is harsh, bright, and often cold.

Death is not a topic that I would have chosen for myself, and I came into it without the bias that infects many other projects. This was a search for me, as well as an assignment to investigate the near-death phenomenon.

Of course, I had heard the term and knew that there were those who claimed to have seen the other side, meaning they believed they had died and left this world. I didn't know that, according to a recent (1992) Gallup Poll, eight million people claimed to have had a near-death experience (NDE). I didn't know that people from other cultures and other countries reported much the same thing when they talked about it at all. And, I didn't realize that there was scientific as well as religious debate over the validity of near-death. Nor did I realize that there was a scientific as well as a Christian bias against acceptance of the NDE.

Studying the phenomenon of the near-death experience provides some insight into what is being reported, but it doesn't actually define the event. The discussion with one man, however does. He had been traveling with a companion when they were caught in a storm of ice and snow. The driver lost control of the car and it slammed into a tree, knocking the driver unconscious but apparently killing the passenger.

For thirty minutes, according to the passenger, he was dead, floating, talking with an uncle who had died years before. Then, with no transition, he was back in the car and fully aware of the danger of his surroundings. He knew that he had to get out of the car and find help. Though gravely injured, he crawled to a house for assistance. There was no doubt in his mind that he had died. He was in the process of transcending this life into the next. For some reason it wasn't time for him to go and he was returned, instantly, to life.

That is his belief. There is no evidence to corroborate it, except for the emergency crew who were surprised that he had lived, given the extent of his injuries, and the facts surrounding the automobile accident.

There are a few examples of those who have died and not returned. Some cases can provide us with insight. My grandmother had been in a coma for a period before she died on a Saturday evening. Before she died, she seemed to be semiconscious and she seemed to see something above her that she wanted to reach. She lifted her arms as if about to embrace someone or something. The impression was that she was staring upward, and trying desperately to reach what she saw above her.

I do not know what she saw because she died right after that . . . moments after that. Because of her illness, no "heroic" effort was made to resuscitate her. That was the right decision to have made at that time given those circumstances.

But her actions give us all something to think about. Did she "see the light" and was she trying to pull herself into the tunnel? Or were these actions just the normal muscle spasms recorded as the electrical activity ceases in the brain? Science might have one answer . . . I have another.

Science, in fact, has done little about near-death until recently. Doctors, psychologists, therapists, and others either ignored the tales or believed them to be nothing more than hallucinations. It was Dr. Raymond Moody who began the interest in near-death and who began the investigations into the circumstances around it.

Moody, author of *Life After Life,* was not the first to record near-death experiences. Pope Gregory the Great included tales of near-death in his *Dialogues.* Though most of the stories in that book seemed to be "morality tales," a number of them included elements of the near-death experience.

The idea, however, that some essential part of the individual survives death is as old as recorded thought. Each culture, each civilization had stories and myths about the "other side" of life. Ancient Egyptians prepared for the journey with gold and food and proper ceremony. Other civilizations believed that the journey was not a one-way trip, but that the soul could be reborn several times . . . in some cases as a lower form of animal but in most as a human, to live another full life.

There is talk that all reference to reincarnation, the idea of the rebirth of the soul, has been edited out of the Bible. Rumors persist that these records are stored in the Vatican, but that Christian teachings require that reincarnation be hidden. Yet, throughout the world, the majority of the people, and the majority of religions, acknowledge reincarnation.

Many Americans now accept reincarnation as true. There are those who engage in "past life" regressions, assisting others in exploring their former lives. Some of them use the techniques to alleviate pain and problems in this life by finding root causes in past lives.

These people are not pushing reincarnation as a religion, but as a fact of life. And there is a body of evidence, much of it anecdotal, that suggests that reincarnation isn't a belief of the unschooled, the ignorant, or the primitive, but something with a foundation in fact. There are stories of reincarnation that have been investigated and corroborated. And, there appears to have been an attempt, both by orthodox religion and the journalistic community to squash the idea without proper investigation.

Many of those reporting past lives claim to have experienced a variety of them. And, contrary to the conventional wisdom, very few suggest they were kings or queens or famous people in a past life. Most report an average life, sometimes rich in detail of how people lived in the past. Many of them had poor, horrible experiences in those past lives.

In fact, if there is a way to learn what happens after death—as opposed to the glimpse that the near-death experiences provide—those who say they have lived before can provide it. They often talk about their death experiences in former lives.

The idea, then, that some part of the individual survives death, is neither new, nor limited. There is a body of evidence to suggest that it happens, and while the hard proof that science demands might not always exist, there is enough evidence to cause questions to be asked. And, there are those who know, because of their personal experiences that such things do happen. They have seen it for themselves, and once a person has had such an experience, no arguments made by others will dissuade them from that belief.

This book is an attempt to put some of these beliefs into perspective. Those who study near-death and reincarnation provide their thoughts. But more importantly, those who have experienced near-death and reincarnation share their insights. Some of the testimony has to be taken on faith . . . but some of it can be corroborated.

There is one important point that must be remembered when reading this work. I have reported, as accurately as I can, the stories related to me. I have not attempted to verify them by checking with relatives, friends, and doctors. In some cases, because of the way things worked, I had the opportunity to learn that those reporting near death had mentioned it many times to others. I have had the opportunity to obtain corroboration, but I did not do so, believing that my task here was to report but not to investigate. All I can do is present the stories as accurately as I possibly can.

The people are real, telling me what they believe to be the truth as they witnessed it. There might be a valid scientific explanation for what they say. Maybe it is, as some have suggested, a function of lack of oxygen to the brain and the subsequent shut-down of various bodily functions in an attempt to save the brain. Maybe it is all a hallucination based on overload to the brain during times of stress, or in this case, as the witness dies . . . or believes that he or she is about to die.

Or maybe it is something else, just as those who have had the experience suggested. Maybe, as they say, they have glimpsed the other side.

Part I:
The Near-Death Experience

One

What is a Near-Death Experience (NDE)?

There are, literally, millions of near-death stories out there. At least eight million people in the United States alone claim to have experienced near-death. Almost everyone knows someone who has had an NDE. The trick is getting them to talk about it. Those who have had the experience are often reluctant to share the story with anyone, including family and friends, because they fear they will not believed. There are those, however, who want to share the experience with all who will listen. They believe that it is something too beautiful to be kept hidden.

Barbara Harris is one of those. Her story has been mentioned in *Psychology Today* (July/August 1992) and *McLean's* (April 20, 1992) and her own book, *Full Circle: The Near-Death Experience and Beyond* (1990). In 1975, Barbara Harris entered the hospital for back surgery but there were complications. She began to bleed internally and her blood pressure dropped dramatically. Instead of fighting to stay alive, she screamed that she wanted to die. She ordered the doctors and nurses to leave her alone. Then she passed out.

Late that night she awoke in the hallway of the hospital. She moved toward her room and realized that she was looking down on her body in bed. A feeling of calm washed over her and the next thing she knew, there was total darkness but she wasn't frightened because she could feel her grandmother, dead for fourteen years, embrace her. She felt a breeze and a low "droning" that was calling her forward. Her next memory is of waking up in the hospital bed.

Betty J. Eadie, with her book *Embraced by the Light* (Gold Leaf Press, 1992), which includes a forward by one of the premier near-death researchers, Dr. Melvin Morse, explored in detail her own NDE and the effects of it on her life. Like many others, she had entered the hospital for surgery and then "died" as a result of it.

It was evening when she turned off the TV in her room, called her husband, and then went to sleep. She awoke, but it seemed that no time had passed. Feeling light-headed, she felt herself seem to slip from her body and then was looking down on a body in bed. She knew that it was dead and then realized that it was her.

There was no fright. She met three beings dressed in robes that she thought were about seventy or eighty, but who were "ancient." She was not afraid, but impressed by the beings. They told her that she had died prematurely.

Eadie then began to worry about her family. She felt that she left the hospital and traveled home, seeing her husband and children, who were unaware of what had happened to her at the hospital. Eadie later wrote that she then "saw" their lives and realized that the children were individuals with their own reasons for being on Earth. Satisfied that they were safe, she returned instantaneously to the hospital where her three friends waited for her.

She was sucked into a dark tunnel and was aware of others, human and animal, traveling with her. Again, she felt no fear, but seemed more interested in what experiences lay in front of her. In the distance was a point of light.

The light grew into something that she described as more brilliant than the sun. Inside was a man, beckoning her forward. She felt a love for him and from him, unlike anything she had ever experienced. Questions flooded her, and she received answers for them. For her, it was a spiritual experience, teaching her many of the purposes of life, and how we all have come to be where we are.

She learned that there were laws that governed all and that much of life, if not all, is predestined. Yet these destinies are selected by those who suffer them, for the experience and growth that comes from them. It is for the learning experience that many of the things happen to us all while we live here on Earth.

Unlike many of those who have had near-death experiences, Eadie was taken beyond the light to explore the "other side," always in the company of one who loved her. She saw many wonders on the other side and described them at length in her own book about NDE.

But Eadie was told that her work had not been completed and she needed to return to her life. It was clear that she wasn't being compelled to return, that the choice was hers and hers alone. At first she refused, employing the tricks that she had learned on Earth during her life to avoid decision. But then she learned what she needed to do if she returned, so the choice would be clearer for her. She then changed her mind and agreed. She would have to return.

She awoke in the hospital, in the cold, heavy human body. Her three friends appeared to her, helped with the transition back into this world. When they left, she noticed that it was about two in the morning. She'd been dead for four hours, but no one at the hospital seemed to have noticed.

Both Barbara Harris and Betty Eadie "died" at night, alone in the hospital. They returned before it was learned they had slipped away. Others have died in emergency rooms, in hospitals, or with others around them, trying desperately to bring them back to life.

Nora Underwood, writing in *McLean's*, told of an orderly in the Chedoke Hospital who suffered a cardiac arrest. When the doctors resuscitated him, he was angry about it. He told Michelle Cooper, a nurse at the hospital, that he thought he had been floating, first through a blackness and then into brightness over a field of clover. He met a brother who had died and who tried to beckon him forward, but instead there was a terrible pain, and he awoke in the emergency room.

When he left the hospital, he contacted a lawyer, arranged his affairs and demanded that he not be resuscitated the next time he was in such a situation. According to Cooper, the man died, but she wasn't bothered by his death because she knew that was what he had wanted.

In their cover story on near-death, *McLean's* also published a firsthand account of the phenomenon. Gilles Bedard had been in the hospital in Montreal, and doctors did not expect him to survive an intestinal disorder. In fact, he was given the last rites. On November 17, 1973, down to seventy-five pounds, he developed a high fever and fell into a coma. He "died" but then came back with a vivid account of what he had seen after he had died.

It was about two in the morning when the doctors turned him to his back. Above him, on the ceiling, was a light that reminded him of the moon. The walls of the room vanished, and Bedard was suddenly looking down on his body. He felt nothing, saying that it "was like watching television." All of that expanded and he saw twelve people standing in a half circle, bathed in a light so bright that it obscured their faces. Bedard didn't recognize any of them, but believed they were waiting for him. They told him that it wasn't his time and that he had a mission to complete on Earth. He didn't have to return, but his life here wasn't finished.

Moments later, Bedard wasn't sure if the event had lasted seconds or as much as half an hour, he was back in his body, but at peace. When he came out of his coma, about five in the morning, he felt good and was ready for a party.

Bedard was not the only one to have a near-death experience when surrounded by doctors. Rev. John Abenschan went into the hospital for a "routine" angioplasty and suffered a heart attack on the operating table. He felt a pain in his chest, and then saw a bright, bell-shaped object over him. The bell descended, covering him and he felt a great inner peace. It is his belief that he was in the "presence of the Lord, Jesus Christ." He said that he was ready to die as the light got brighter. Instead, he awoke in a hospital room.

Disappointed to discover that he wasn't in heaven, he said he "fussed" at the Lord. The inner peace returned and he knew that it hadn't been his time.

Abenschan said that he had always believed in a life after death but had wondered if he would surrender to it or if he would fight. The experience answered the question for him. It did not, as some claim, change his outlook on death or dying, but strengthened his faith.

The doctors were concerned that he would not survive his stay in the hospital, but he knew he would. He'd seen the light and the Lord and knew that it wasn't his time.

Abenschan is convinced that he "died." According to the doctors his blood pressure dropped so that it was nearly nonexistent and they suggested he had "died" while undergoing the medical procedure. They believed he had been clinically dead for a short period of time.

One of the strangest of the near-death experiences is one that could corroborate some of the detail of them and provide some interesting proof for them. Unfortunately it is a second-hand story, lacking the names of the principals or where they were from. Lori Erickson reported in the *Iowa City Press-Citizen* that she had spoken to a patient who told her, "Something happened to a friend of mine that I think might interest you. I never believed in ghosts before, but I trust my friend and he swears it's true."

The friend had been in a terrible car accident, but before he regained consciousness in the hospital, he had seen himself walking across a meadow. Soon he was joined by a young woman he'd never seen before. As he spoke to her, he noticed that she had been badly hurt. Blood stained her clothes and there were bruises on her face and arms. Looking at himself, he saw that he too, was covered with blood.

He felt no pain and the woman seemed to be in none. They spoke, sharing their names and other details of their lives. She was from a small town in Wisconsin.

As they continued across the field, he noticed that her wounds seemed to be healing themselves until all her injuries were gone. His weren't healing. He was still covered with blood. At that moment, he realized that she was going to "die" and he was going to survive.

He woke up in the hospital and did survive his injuries, undergoing a long, painful process of rehabilitation. Months later, driving through Wisconsin, he recognized the name of the small town and stopped at the local library to read the back issues of the newspaper. He found the obituary of the young woman who had died in a car wreck on the same day as his own nearly fatal traffic accident.

It wouldn't be fair to recount this NDE without qualifying it. There are no names attached to it so that records can't be independently verified. That doesn't mean it didn't happen. But until there is a way to verify this account, it should be considered, with the qualification that it is not from a firsthand source.

These examples of the near-death experience reveal some of the commonality among those who have had such episodes. However, prior to the mid-1970s, no one had discussed, publicly, near-death. A few people, mostly doctors, had heard tales of NDE, but had dismissed them as hallucinations and delusions induced either by the drugs given to patients, or as the result of the trauma of extreme medical procedures and of nearly dying from them. Doctors just weren't interested in pursuing the reports.

The exception was Raymond Moody. In *The Light Beyond* (Bantam Books, 1988) he recalled that he first learned about near-death as a philosophy major in college. In the course of that study, he learned of Dr. George Ritchie, who told of dying, glimpsing the afterlife and then returning to the Earth. Moody thought little about it, filing it away.

Later, after Moody earned his doctorate and was teaching philosophy himself, he learned that one of his students had experienced a near-death event. When he questioned his student, he discovered that those experiences matched, generally, those of George Ritchie. By the time Moody decided he wanted to go to medical school, he had collected a number of near-death stories from individuals he considered "reliable, sincere people."

In medical school he found that many doctors claimed they had never heard of a near-death experience although they had "resuscitated" hundreds of people. Other doctors claimed it was a form of mental illness. In fact, Moody found a laundry list of excuses provided by the doctors—ranging from the fact they believed only the religious experienced NDE to a belief that children, unpolluted by cultural bias, never reported near death.

Dr. Melvin Morse, a pediatrician in Seattle, was able to refute one of those claims. In "Children of the Light," printed in *Reader's Digest* (from his book, *Closer to the Light*, Villard Books, a division of Random House, 1992), he told of "Katie" a seven-year-old who had been found floating face down in a pool. Morse was sure she would die, but instead, she recovered, telling Morse, in precise detail, who had come into the emergency room in their attempts to save her life. She remembered being taken into X-ray and she recalled the procedures preformed there.

Under questioning by Morse, the girl revealed that there had been darkness until a tunnel opened and a woman appeared. She accompanied Katie up the tunnel where she met her late grandfather. Katie also recalled meeting the "Heavenly Father" and Jesus. When Jesus asked if she wanted to see her family again, she said yes. Almost immediately, she awakened.

In fact, the majority of objections raised by those other doctors is just the sort of myth-making that inhibits free thought. They are able to rationalize away something that they don't want to acknowledge. If it can be labeled in rational terms as a hallucination, a delusion, or the ramblings of the overly religious, then it is not something that has to be studied or considered. Once labeled it can be filed away and never looked at again.

But Moody was fascinated. He eventually interviewed dozens of people who reported NDEs. That allowed him to create a list of common reported experiences: events and observations that were mentioned by most of those who returned from the brink of death. To him, it suggested that there was something more than just the ramblings of sick people and the mentally ill.

Moody warns that no two experiences are exactly the same, but that a few of them come remarkably close. No one has ever related all of the components of the "complete" near-death experience as Moody has developed them, but a few have mentioned the majority of them. No one component is found in all the events. But there is not a single event that has only appeared in a single experience. In other words, each of the components has appeared in several of the accounts.

With that in mind, an examination of the

elements of the near-death experience might be illustrative. It will establish a core of knowledge that will facilitate understanding.

First on Moody's list is *Ineffability*. This means simply, that those who have had the experience fail to find the proper words to explain it. My own research has borne this out as each of those I spoke to repeated that they just couldn't find the right words to describe what they were attempting to tell me. Language failed to provide them with the proper words for description. Tom Dolembo, who is a part-time writer, even admitted this, something a writer should never do. A writer should always be able to find the proper words.

Many of those who have had NDEs say that they heard themselves pronounced dead. Sometimes it is done by doctors in attendance, other times by family, friends, or bystanders. According to Moody, one man, the victim of a car accident heard someone ask if he was dead. Another voice said, "Yeah. He's dead."

Most everyone talks of being at peace and feeling calm. Though it seems that the near-death experience should be frightening, that is rarely the result. Initial fear is replaced with a warm feeling of love and calm and a belief that they are at peace.

There are those who speak of a great deal of noise. Some say it is a "rushing" sound. Others report music. Bedard said that he heard music. Later he met a man who also had a near-death experience and was trying to reproduce the music he heard while in the light.

Fifth on Moody's list is the out-of-body experience. Many of those report a floating sensation and that they then look down at the scene. They can, after resuscitation or reviving, describe the scenes around them. Some talk of returning home to see family and friends one last time. They can, it seems, move around the physical world quickly and easily, but they are invisible to those inhabiting the world.

One man, Chet Szeliga, did more than move around the world, he escaped it, finding himself in space, looking down at the Earth. He described it as looking at the Earth from the moon, almost as if in that famous picture of a crescent Earth in the sky above the moon. He could see no continental shape, just the oceans and clouds obscuring the planet.

Like the others, he was at peace and unafraid. He saw no one else, heard nothing, and he awoke in the hospital, convinced that he had died.

Nearly all NDEs include meeting someone to assist them in the transition from life to death—many times a friend or relative who had died sometime before. This also often has a calming effect.

There are those who speak of a being of light. According to Moody, this is as close as he comes to a universal in the near-death experience. Moody also writes that this has the most profound effect on people. The being of light is described as a being of pure love, a being of brilliant light where the face is obscured; some people with a Christian heritage identify this as Christ.

The being of light then begins a communication with those it wants to assist. There may be questions asked of it and it may provide the answers, or it asks if the person is now ready to die.

After the appearance of the being of light comes a review of the life just lived. Unlike normal memory, the review is rapid, as if flashed on a screen to be seen sometimes reported in color or three-dimensional vision. There seems to be nothing upsetting, it is a review of the earliest "memories" of life up to the point of death. There is nothing judgmental about the past-life review. It is just that . . . a review.

As the people progress through the near-death experience they reach a limit or border, according to Moody. Some have suggested they are at a gate and paradise is on the other side of that gate. Some have described the limit as a gray wall or a mist or even just a line in front of them.

Some of those have suggested that they are asked if they are prepared to die. Others say that they are told early in their experience that it is a mistake, that there is something left to be done in their life. They are still on the "wrong" side of the light and can't see beyond it.

Many of those who have reached this point have no desire to return. They want to stay with the being of light, or progress farther into the realm. It is suggested that they must return, though some are given a choice. Moody reports that some women with young children at home, felt an obligation to return for their children. Others are told there is a mission for them. Betty Eadie was shown more about her life so that she could make a more intelligent decision about her return.

Once they have returned, each of those experiencing near-death, must decide whether or not to tell about it. Certain of them, such as Tom Dolembo, keep the story secret for years but gradually begin sharing it with friends. Moody reports that others learn quickly that the rest of the world isn't all that interested. There are the skeptics who question everything.

Nearly all of those who experience near-death report they were profoundly changed by the event. Issues, activities, goals that had once seemed important are modified or changed. Now living life is important.

They report that they are no longer afraid of death. Some talk of a fear of the process of dying. Once the dying is finished, "being dead" is wonderful. One man described the lingering death of his father because of cancer. The prospect of dying such a horrible death is frightening to him, but he knows what lies beyond that pain if he is forced to suffer it.

Moody's last point is corroboration. Many of those who have near-death experiences talk of out-of-body travel. They have the opportunity to see family members one last time. This provides one area that can be corroborated. If they are correct about what is happening miles from the hospital or accident site or scene of their death, then a level of corroboration can be achieved.

Eadie, for example, traveled from the hospital, returning to her home miles from the hospital to see her husband reading the newspaper and the children in the process of going to bed. By questioning family members, it is possible to learn if the activities described were accurate.

Moody writes of patients who are able to tell doctors, nurses and emergency room personnel exactly what happened to them. Many tell of the words spoken after they have been pronounced dead.

This proves that the impressions of the scene around them were accurate. And it suggests that some sort of out-of-body travel has taken place. Unfortunately, this is about all that is available in the way of corroboration.

What Moody and other researchers, as well as writers, have discovered is that there is a real phenomenon surrounding the belief in near-death. Since Moody published *Life After Life* there has been discussion of it in all forms of the media, but it is clear that many people experienced near-death long before Moody reported on it. Many of these people had shared their experiences with friends and family before they knew that others had experienced the same things.

The consensus seems to be that there is a near-death phenomenon. There are, literally, millions of witnesses to it, and there are several doctors studying it carefully. In fact, there is no question that there is something to these stories. The question seems to no longer be whether or not near-death exists, but what it is.

Two

Tom Dolembo

To understand the near-death phenomenon completely it is necessary to examine the case histories in depth. A brief survey provides interesting information, but it is only after speaking to those who have had the experience that the true nature of near-death can be understood fully. It is clear, from these people, that they are providing a story that they believe to be the truth. There is no question that they are relating, accurately, their own experience.

Many of the stories begin with a traumatic event. Some have suffered fatal illness, a heart attack, died on the operating table, or they have been in terrible accidents. Tom Dolembo, a passenger in a Volkswagen, was killed in a traffic accident.

Dolembo, at the time, was twenty-one years old and a student at Harvard. He was interested in all sorts of activities that "took him to the edge." He planned to enroll in the Marine

Platoon Leader's Class, an ROTC function at Harvard. He envisioned himself as a second lieutenant fighting Communism in Vietnam. But that was all in the future. At the time he died, he and a friend were on a rock-climbing expedition to Mt. Katahdin, in northern Maine. It was late winter, sometime in March, but the weather was cold and snowy. The roads in Maine were treacherous with sleet and ice. According to Dolembo, the weather was going from bad to worse but there was no other traffic. The road belonged to them.

Dolembo was in the passenger's seat, dozing. The driver hit a patch of black ice on the road, the car swerved, and they slammed into a tree. Dolembo hit the dashboard and then the windshield, snapping his neck, apparently killing him. Later, from doctors, he would learn that he had suffered multiple head injuries, he had "stripped" the skin of his face away from the bone, the fifth cervical vertebra was snapped, and his spinal cord was heavily damaged.

There was no period of transition for him. He had been dozing in the front seat and suddenly he had been critically injured in the accident. "During the period of time in which . . . I can remember this very vividly . . . during the time . . . I don't know where I was. I can't really describe where I was. There was no pain . . . I know the color was generally gray around me."

He said that he could not feel his arms or

legs, and that he was aware of having a body, but he couldn't see it. He looked for a body but couldn't find it. "I felt as if I had one," he said. "That seems kind of ridiculous."

Dolembo moved along "in this place wherever it was . . ." He felt that he was moving and judged time, not in the passage of minutes, but with the passage of distance. He felt suspended someplace but moving through it.

"I did have a sense that time was passing," said Dolembo, "that I was spending time in this place. It seemed like a long time actually."

Dolembo found himself, not in a tunnel as described by so many others, but in a very large room with gray walls. Not shades of gray, but a single, uniform color. The walls had texture, like velvet, but that was just an observation because he could not touch it.

The room itself was like a vault that was dome-shaped. Dolembo thought there was a dome over his head. He didn't notice if there was anything like a floor under his feet because he didn't look down at any time. He was in a room of uniform gray with no sign of a mist or a fog near him. There was nothing else in the room until a brilliant light opened up in front of him.

Dolembo said, "It was just there. I didn't move toward it. It didn't move toward me. It was just like someone had switched a light on right in front of me." It was a brilliant light, more like a sheet of light than a single point.

Following quickly, Dolembo was aware of a voice, either hearing it or feeling it, but he found it hard to describe. It seemed to be coming from the light. "I didn't hear anyone speak exactly, but I knew that someone was communicating with me very clearly and directly. I tried to see a face but I couldn't. It sounded very much like an uncle of mine."

The voice, according to Dolembo, was familiar, but it was from someone who had died several years before. "It was a familiar voice from someone who was not alive . . . there was a very distinct Chicago accent. It didn't sound like anyone else."

Dolembo hadn't moved very far, into this . . . place as he describes it. There was a voice of an uncle, and he, Dolembo "was confronting this person."

"I know that I had a kind of conversation, but it was very direct. Number one was I had a lot of questions that I had unanswered and that was why I was behaving the way I was . . . rock climbing and building climbing at home."

Dolembo wanted it made clear that at this point in his life, his priorities were set in a single direction. He was searching for danger, taking up those things that provided danger and that could take him to the "edge of life." That was why he was rock climbing and why he had entertained thoughts of being a Marine officer with a tour in Vietnam.

"What happened," said Dolembo, "this is going to sound really strange. Before this happened I was just . . . I had these millions of questions to ask and in an instant they were all literally answered. The meaning of life and all . . ."

That experience, as close as he could describe it, was as if information had been down-loaded from a computer. "Before this happened I had all these burning questions and it's like someone said, 'Oh, I can handle that.' That was the sense I got but not the words. And then I got this instantaneous, the best I can tell you that I got this download that said, 'Okay, if that's what's causing you to behave this way, here, bang, take this and now you don't have to do this.' "

The flow of information continued. "Immediately . . . everything I was doing before ceased. I just didn't have those questions anymore. They were just gone. They were answered. I can't tell you the meaning of life . . . It wasn't religious. I didn't meet any religious people. I couldn't tell you that I saw angels or anything like that. [It] was like I met my uncle who then said, 'Okay . . . these are the answers.' "

Then came the surprise. Dolembo said, "It was really kind of funny. There was this pause like is there anything else. I, at that point had no more questions to ask and then this presence just told me very directly that 'Life is not that serious. It's not about that. Chill out.' "

"The thing that I still remember," said Dolembo, "is this very funny person saying, 'Look, it wouldn't look like this if it was serious. If it was meant to have meaning it wouldn't look like this."

Dolembo was a little confused because the voice, still sounding very much like his uncle seemed to be a little bit more profound than his uncle had ever been. Dolembo stressed this. He wanted it clearly understood that the sense he got from the voice was that life was not meant to be taken so seriously. It was funny. Something to be enjoyed and that to be on the edge of life and death, to constantly stretch over the edge to see what was out there, was not the way to do it. Life was not serious. There was a lot of misery in the world, but it was created by those living their lives and was unnecessary. The uncle's voice told him, "You don't have to be serious about it."

It wasn't a comedian talking to him, trying to make a joke out of everything. It was just a very funny being trying to help him out. "I got a sense of . . . everything was pretty well taken care of without my having to be concerned about it . . . whatever I was doing to risk my life . . . was not really doing me or anybody any good and it wasn't going to happen.

Whatever was going to happen was going to happen to me. I might as well just accept it. What I was doing was just crazy. It was for the wrong purpose . . . in the wrong direction. It was like somebody brought me up short. They said to me and I got very clearly, 'Everything's going to be okay.' "

And then Dolembo woke up. No transition, no time to get ready to return to Earth. He woke up in the wrecked car, soaked in gasoline and aware that the ignition to the engine was on. The engine had stopped but the lights were still burning. Dolembo was bleeding from his injuries and his friend, the driver, was still unconscious.

Although he knew he was badly hurt, and aware of the gasoline around him, he still had this feeling of great inner peace. He'd been told that everything was going to be fine. It would be all right.

He kicked at the door, finally forcing it open and pulled himself out, falling to the sleet- and snow-covered ground. There was a sudden, intense pain in his neck and he grabbed his jaw, forcing his head back, locking his hand in place under his chin. Dolembo said that he didn't know why he did it, he just knew that he had to.

Afraid of a sudden fire, he dragged himself away from the smashed car and then, with his free hand, he pulled himself along the pavement, crawling along the road like a snake. In the distance was a dark house, and Dolembo began the long journey toward it, through the continuing sleet, his hand forcing his head up and back, locked in place. He remembered a loud voice telling him to push hard on his neck. That he wasn't to let go of his neck under any circumstances.

He described that voice, a sort of internal voice that was very loud, telling him repeatedly, almost shouting at him, not to move his hand away from his jaw. He said, "There was nothing peaceful about it. It was awful and it was like . . . I just knew vividly that that [holding his hand under his jaw] was what I had to do."

Movement was difficult with one hand jammed up under his neck. Scrambling like a bug, he reached the steps of the house about forty-five minutes later and crawled up them, but has no conscious memory of ringing the bell or knocking on the door. He said, "I don't know how the door got answered." A girl, ten or twelve, was suddenly standing there. Dolembo remembered, "She was cool."

Dolembo said, ". . . all I remember is somebody coming out and asking what was wrong . . . I didn't say anything but it was pretty clear."

He had managed to reach a mortuary in the small town of Millinocket, Maine, but the mortuary's ambulance was out on another run. Dolembo doesn't remember much of the next several minutes, just that he refused to take his hand away from his neck. "They literally," he said, "had to pry my hand [away]."

Later one of the doctors in the hospital told him, "If you hadn't done that the first thing, the medical people would . . . yank your head back and opened your throat and that would have snapped your spinal cord."

Later, in the hospital, one of the doctors asked him how he felt and Dolembo responded, "I can't feel anything." He had lost all feeling in his body.

At that point, according to him, the feeling started to drop away from his body. This was not part of an out-of-body experience. It was the result of the injuries that he had suffered in the crash.

Although the medical staff was worried about the fading feelings, Dolembo told them not to worry. He was going to be fine. Everything was going to be fine. The doctor cautioned him about being overly optimistic. They told him that the fact he'd had feeling when they brought him in was a good sign, but the fact it was fading was not so good. The doctor said, ". . . the odds of your coming out of this . . . there is a good chance this has traumatized your spinal cord and you might never get it [feeling] back again."

Dolembo didn't care what the doctor, or anyone else, said, because he knew the truth. He

said, "Don't worry about it, Doc, it'll be fine."
Dolembo knew there was nothing for him to
worry about.

According to Dolembo about two nights
later the guy in the bed next to him called the
doctor to complain about Dolembo. The patient said that Dolembo was getting up from
his bed and walking around the room all the
time. That bothered him and he wanted it to
stop.

But Dolembo was on pain killers, unconscious most of the time, and, the doctor told
the other patient that Dolembo couldn't walk.
"He's paralyzed," the doctor said.

"The heck he can't," said the man.

At that point the doctor tested each of Dolembo's limbs. He said, "You can feel things."
When Dolembo confirmed it, the doctor said,
"I think you're going to be okay. I wouldn't
have bet this in a million years because of the
X-rays . . . we're going to leave you in the position you're in now . . . no surgery or nothing."

Dolembo spent another two weeks in the
Millinocket hospital, a month at Harvard in the
health center there, and then returned to his
home in Michigan City, Indiana, for about two
years of convalescence and therapy. He was no
longer interested in rock and building climbing
or any of the other dangerous activities that
had attracted him before the accident.

While he was home to allow himself to heal, the local draft board called him up for military service, because he was no longer protected by the ROTC or a college deferment. When he reported to the draft board, he told them that he had broken his neck, but military doctors and clerks had heard every excuse imaginable to keep someone out of military service. Dolembo had to go through the whole physical but when he finished, "the guy looked at my X-ray and says, 'You shouldn't be on your feet for so long . . . you broke your neck.' [I mentioned] 'We'd talked about that like nine hours ago' [and he said], 'Oh, yeah, I remember you.' They just said, 'No, that's okay. You don't have to [go].'"

Today, Dolembo has recovered completely from his injuries. They didn't affect his life the way they could have. There was a massive trauma to his body, but he was never concerned about it because he knew that it was all going to be fine. He'd been told that while he was dead. His uncle, or the voice of the light, had assured him that he would survive and that he would recover.

Dolembo believes that he was dead for a period of time. There is no question in his mind about it. For a short period after the crash, he was dead.

The most profound changes, however, were in his attitude. Dolembo said, "Actually, I think it changed who I was radically. It was like a hundred-and-eighty degree reversal."

After the experience, he had no desire to be a Marine or to go to Vietnam. "I went through the motions when I got drafted because I knew that it would not happen."

And he never went rock climbing again. "I didn't go to church any more often. I didn't have a sense of God and it's not like there was a saint . . . [It was] very personal. It was like family."

Dolembo didn't get a feeling that it wasn't his time to die, or that his death had been premature. He said, "The closest I got was the sense that everything was going to be okay. [That I] didn't have to worry about coming now . . . everything is going to be all right. It was . . . made quite clear that whatever I had to go through may be not easy but [that I] could handle it. It's not a big deal.

"It's like someone had showed me but I can't really describe it but someone showed me the entire rest of my life . . . It [death, or life] isn't something that you have to rush . . . It isn't that I can describe . . . what the rest of my life is going to be but it's like my uncertainty of the future ended. It literally ended in terms of what am I going to do. It isn't that I haven't had periods of normal remorse. It's as if the great questions of life [were answered for me].

That's out of the way. I still have to make a living."

But the answers to the great questions were simple, according to Dolembo. He now knows that "It [life] it's not very serious. It does just kind of happen. I'm absolutely convinced that the more I see of life, the less it has to do with achievement and wealth . . . The more it has to do with . . . the only thing I had when I went through that experience was some loved one's voice on the other side. That must be all that's worth [anything] . . . so the rest of it is just silly."

According to him, relationships with other people are important. "It's pretty much how it was done to me in that light . . . how much we can do in this life rather than wait for someone to bang us in the head . . . It would be a much nicer world if that were true . . . and it seems that that is where things go . . . what's left [after death] is what pieces of us were kind . . . The rest just belongs [left behind] . . . This was very personal. I just talked to someone who knew all the answers and who was already there. I didn't get a sense of profound knowledge . . . [I got] real personal reassurances . . . like [what] someone would tell a loved one."

Dolembo also said that he had a "heightened sense of things that will happen. . . . I [can't] predict the future but it's . . . [I can] anticipate bad things happening. I seem to have a heightened sense of things happening. I haven't got any idea what they're going to be . . . when things are going to happen that are momentous, I have a real sense that they are happening."

Dolembo was clear that his experience had not made him a religious person. He said, "I've always had a little bit of religion in me but I can't say it made me a religious person. I think I can relate to a lot of what is said [in the Bible] now much better. I know what love is."

That was a theme that he came back to frequently, stressing that it was love, and maybe the good in a person, that survived after death. He said, ". . . what happens is that everything is stripped away except love. A lot of people have a lot of other things they carry with them all the time . . . anger and all the crazy [ideas]. Everybody has this core of love and in the end that's all that's left. The rest of it belongs here [on the Earth]. That's the hard part to understand. You can't just say I'm going to become a really good person now or I'm going to do all these things that are good because you can't say that. You can't prepare for something like this. All that I know is that the only part that remains is the part that is love . . . I'm convinced of that."

He continued, saying, "You take the good you had here and you leave the rest behind. I don't know what to tell people who ask, 'Yeah. What about Hitler?' I mean, I don't know what to tell people but all I know is that my sense is from what I saw that's what happens and that, if that's what happens, what's so bad about that?"

But Dolembo had an observation about the experience. "The interesting part . . . it wasn't a presence, it was a relative . . . so whatever it was, either in my mind or in my memory or whatever, it was a meeting. He had an identity and so did I. I didn't lose that. I didn't lose my identity. I was still me. The body and everything else I'm not sure about. I know that I had an identity. I know that it was exactly the one that I took into it."

The experience had other effects on Dolembo. He said that he became a worse student. "I went to Harvard business school and I did really well, but I'm afraid when the time came between a nice day and my books, I went to the river and slept on the riverbank. I still have . . . that's a terrible habit, but I still have it."

It changed his perception of death. Dolembo believes that he was dead for a time, but there is no way to prove it. He added, "If I'm alive now, I must not have been dead, but I was real close." But it did alter his perception and he no longer fears it.

Dolembo said, "My father died last year. We knew he was dying." Unfortunately, Dolembo wasn't able to communicate to him the experiences he'd had so long ago.

He said, "I really think that what you're going toward is wonderful and I can't describe to you how wonderful it is. But he [Dolembo's father] was a tough old bird. I think, toward the end, we had a communication. I didn't want to scare the living crap out of him."

Interestingly, Dolembo said, "I'm not sure that I would come to terms with it any better than anyone else dying. That's a whole different thing. I watched him die. That was not pleasant. I don't know what it was like for him but it was not pleasant [watching him die] for me. But death, that's really pretty wonderful. It's something that you don't want to rush but it's something that when it happens naturally, I don't think you want to fling yourself out the window to see the light . . . That's not what happens, but it is . . . natural . . . it's the only way that everything makes sense."

He added, "The process of dying is a little awesome . . . the dead part of it is actually pretty wonderful."

Dolembo said that you move onto a better realm. One where you take the good and leave the bad behind. A realm where there is a sense of identity and of being, but with the problems and worries of Earth stripped away.

For Dolembo, this was a growth experience. "I think that anybody who says that on Sunday morning you're going to find God in church . . . I think it depends on the day . . . I hate to say that but I kind of [believe] that every day is so precious and beautiful that you can't waste them. That part of it was a gift. That's a wonderful gift. One thing I wasn't aware of was whether or not on the other side of the light was there a lake. All I can say was that on the other side of the light . . . I don't know . . . it was just there. I feel a very intense need to just enjoy [every-day life].

Dolembo doesn't know if he had been physically, or clinically dead. Asked about it, he said, "I don't know . . . They said at that time there was no way of telling my physical condition . . . a severe shocked condition . . . I would say that I was close. Definitely, I was close. I . . . expect to see that same thing when I die."

One of his regrets was that he was unable to communicate the beauty of his experience to his father as he was dying. During the last three weeks of his life, Dolembo noticed that his father was more relaxed. Maybe he had accepted his fate, or maybe he had had a glimpse of the other side.

He said, "There were two people who helped. One was a carpenter who showed up to fix the front porch . . . and then a black woman named Ester who was with my dad until he died . . . That was a kind of interesting twist."

Dolembo added, "I wish I could have communicated it better but it sounds crazy when you tell people . . . If you talk about it, they get this sort of funny, distant look in their eyes and sort of want to know if you've had your medication. You learn not to talk about it. I talked about it a couple of times. He [the father] got this sort of worried look in his face. He didn't need that. I'm not sure that he had the same experience at all. I have no idea."

When he was asked if there was anything that stuck out, he said, "Actually, the strange thing is that I sort of laugh every time I think about it . . . whatever it was, it was very funny. I'm not really sure what else went on, but all I can remember when I think about it is laughing. It was funny. Whatever was going on was much funnier than I can even remember. It was at least as funny as anything I have ever seen. And it was probably seeing life in perspective for about five minutes is pretty amusing. Somebody who is not in this, looking at what we do everyday, has got [to find this as] one of the most amusing things in the world. That's got to be funny."

Dolembo, in his experience, related many of the things that others have observed. But when he "died" it was the late 1960s and no one was talking about near-death experiences. When it happened to him, he had no idea that others had experienced the same thing. It wasn't until the mid-1970s that he read, for the first time, about the near-death phenomenon. To him, it meant that he was not alone in his feelings and his belief. Others had been to the same place, seen the same things.

Dolembo described himself as "the world's biggest pessimist, but it's got a soft core to it. It doesn't matter anyway. Things happen without my eternal presence. It's a little hard to keep up the front. Whatever went on was funny."

Dolembo said that he believed this was a miracle. "I personally believe it . . . not the greatest in history, but the greatest in my history."

Three

Sarah Ward

There really is no such thing as routine surgery. As doctors caution, every procedure, no matter how minor, has its risks and possible complications. Any time a knife is used or the patient must undergo anesthesia, there is the possibility that something can go wrong.

Sarah Ward, a thirty-five-year-old mother of three hadn't worried about the minor surgery to correct a lower back problem. For a year or more she'd put up with the pain and the inability to walk more than fifty yards without her back beginning to hurt. But then one day it got suddenly worse. She couldn't stand, sit or lie comfortably. After tossing in bed for half an hour, she would finally discover a position that worked, only to have to move in ten minutes and begin the procedure over again. She couldn't sleep and the pain was intense.

The doctor told her that there was no longer any choice. The problem had deteriorated to the point where only surgery could correct it. Pain-killers, chiropractors, and simple endurance were no longer options. She had to "go under the knife."

She wasn't worried about it and actually looked forward to the procedure because it promised relief. As she went through the routine of checking into the hospital, undergoing the preparations for surgery, and the final trip down the cold, sterile hall she felt a sense of dread but put it down to nerves because she was about to have an operation. Then she was inside the operating room, and everything was fading away as the anesthetic began to work rapidly.

During the procedure, something went wrong, and Sarah Ward died. Her first memory and experience was not of waking in the recovery room as it is for most patients. She suddenly heard the doctors talking quietly, an urgency in their voices. Something fell to the floor with a clatter but they ignored it.

She was aware of light and then was above the scene, looking down, as the doctors struggled to resuscitate her. They worked around her chest, massaging it, as they struggled to find a heartbeat. The activity around the body on the table was interesting but she didn't really care about it. When she realized that they were working on her body, apparently dead, her attitude didn't change markedly. She saw the event as interesting, in a detached sort of way.

Although she realized that she was dead, that didn't concern her either because there were other things happening around her. There was a bright light in the distance. A pinpoint of brightness that looked like one of those large lamps above the operating table seen from a great distance at night. The pinpoint of brightness drew her attention.

There was a ringing sound filling her head. She didn't know if it was some sort of alarm because of what was happening inside the operating room, or if it was something from the outside, where she seemed to be drifting. But the ringing got louder, seeming to be more insistent, as if it was trying to tell her something.

Now she focused on the light and thought that it was moving toward her, growing brighter. But the surroundings began to fade. She lost sight of the operating room and the doctors and nurses. All she could see was the light, growing brighter and larger. She realized that it was not coming toward her, but she was approaching it.

"I knew that I had to get there," she said. "I wanted to get to that light. It seemed to be that it . . . offered sanctuary. If I could get to it, I would be safe."

Ward found herself surrounded by black. "It looked like I was in a tunnel, but I wasn't standing on anything . . . I was floating, wanting to move to the light."

She was aware of something inside the light, at first a speck that marred the perfect brightness of it. To Ward, it looked like an insect on a light bulb, but as she got closer, it began to take shape.

"I think that I was moving . . . I was going deeper into the tunnel . . . I didn't think to look back. I now wonder if I would have seen the operating room if I looked back. But then, I was more interested in what was in front of me."

The sides of the tunnel, and the top of it began to fade as the light expanded outward. The speck grew larger, beginning to look like a human. Ward could see the outline of a body, though details were impossible to make out because the light was so bright.

She didn't know if she'd stopped moving or if the light had stopped growing but the scene didn't change, only the ringing ended, fading away. She stayed where she was, unworried, because the light seemed to have a warm, friendly glow to it. She had the impression that she was in the presence of something holy. She wasn't sure that she wanted to call it God, but she felt humbled by it.

"I studied the figure but I couldn't see the face. I couldn't see fingers on the hands either and was concerned about that. But it might have been that the light was so bright . . . the little details were washed out."

The shape lifted a hand and began to talk to her. "I don't know if it spoke out loud. I heard the words forming . . . I guess you could say in my head. It was a calming voice . . . pleasant . . . and comforting."

The shape grew larger, coming toward her. "I was filled with love . . . this person . . . I don't know what else to call it, seemed to be radiating love and peace. I wanted to go forward to join in. I was ready to join it."

Now she seemed to slip deeper into the tunnel, sucked into it, toward the light. "I don't know who it was. I just felt incredibly relaxed and knew that I had died . . . I felt some regret because of things I wanted to say to my husband and kids . . . I didn't like leaving them so unexpectedly . . . that was in the corner of my mind, just there as a reminder of what I had back in this world. A very gentle reminder."

With the "being of the light" she continued deeper into the tunnel, her mind filled with questions. "There was so much I wanted to know . . . I hoped that my family would be all right without me. I wanted to know what had happened to me and what heaven would be like . . ."

They entered a room of astonishing brightness. "It was like a waiting room, though I didn't see anyone else waiting there. The . . .

being with me faded away. I don't know if he went through another door or just disappeared . . . I was left alone in this room. A huge room . . . There had to be walls, but I couldn't really see them. I was just sort of aware of them . . . far in front of me was a door . . . This is hard to describe . . . I knew the door was there, but I couldn't really see it. I thought that if I could, I could enter heaven, but the door was sort of vague . . . faint, as if someone had drawn it on the wall with a light pencil. Such a faint outline that I wasn't even sure that it was there . . . I had an impression of a door.

"This was very critical," she said. "I knew that . . . my future depended on my seeing the door. I wondered if I was going to need glasses because I just couldn't make it out. No matter how hard I tried, I couldn't see it clearly and I was disappointed in myself."

Ward wanted it understood that all during this experience, her major feeling was of calm and relaxation. "I was completely at peace with myself . . . I was aware of these other feelings but they weren't all that important . . . It's hard to make people understand that the major feeling was peace and an inner calm, but I had other emotions . . . other feelings but the overwhelming feeling was peace. I was blissfully happy even though I couldn't see the door well. I knew that it was important to see the door, and as I stared at it, I thought it was becoming sharper . . . but it wasn't all that important.''

She stayed in the room for a period of time. According to her, time had no real meaning. There had to be a passage of time, but, as Ward said, "Time meant nothing there. A minute or a day. Time has no meaning.''

Then a feeling of sadness seemed to wrap around her. "Nothing had changed that I could see . . . but I was suddenly unhappy. I heard a voice tell me that it was not time . . . that was why I couldn't see the door properly.

"Now I wanted to see that door. I stared at it, focusing my attention on it, but I couldn't see it any better. I had to see that door and all the time I knew that something was wrong. Someone had made a mistake.''

The being that she had seen earlier reappeared, now seeming to move in the other direction. "This time I didn't want to follow but I knew that I had to . . . the room disappeared and the light faded until it was just a pinpoint again. Then I was in the recovery room . . . in bright lights but I knew right away where I was.''

As she lay in the recovery room, she was thinking about what had happened. She knew that she had died and for some reason she had come back. There had been no reason for it given, other than a mistake had been made.

"I've since read about these near-death experiences so I know something about what happens. What I saw differed somewhat, but what strikes me is that these others were given a choice. They were told it was too early for them to die but they could continue if they wanted. I didn't have a choice. I knew I had been . . . what, rejected. I was sad at having to return. I wasn't told that I needed to do something more in my life. It was made clear to me that I had to return. There was just no opportunity for a choice."

Later, in talking to her doctor, she asked what had happened during the operation. He was startled by the question but told Ward there had been a reaction to the anesthetic. There had been some tense moments as her heartbeat became erratic. Technically, she had died, though she had a heartbeat and respiration throughout the trouble. It had lasted less than a minute according to the medical records and to the doctors who had been there.

"I am sure that I was dead," she said. "When I told the doctor what I had seen inside the operating room, he said that I was right. The procedures, the techniques, were the ones they had used. That was the sense of urgency that I felt . . . but they were never panicked. They were all doing their jobs in a professional, competent manner."

Grinning, she said, "I since wondered that

if we sued over this, if I could give testimony to the court. I was there, but according to the doctors, I was unconscious. But I knew what was going on around me. I could tell them who was doing what. It would have been an interesting test case in court. Can a patient who is under the influence of an anesthetic testify to what happened? If drunks are allowed to testify to what happened while they were drunk, why couldn't I?"

Like so many of the others who have had such experiences, Ward said that she learned many things during the short period that she was dead. She realized that relationships with family and friends are very important. Her major regret was not having told her husband that she loved him or that she hadn't told her children to be good and to think of her once in a while. Had she not returned, that was the thing that would have bothered her.

But other than that, she was profoundly moved by the experience. Again, like so many others, she knows that something lies beyond life. That death does not mean the end of everything, but is a new beginning Death is a transition from one aspect of "life" into another.

"I am sure that what I saw was what happens after we die. I believe that we are confronted by that which will make us the most comfortable. I've been lucky that I've had no close family members or friends die. There was no one to meet me there that I would recognize. I think that was why I saw . . . I hesitate to say it . . . but I think I saw God . . . That makes me sound like a nut case, but that's the impression I got . . . Maybe it wasn't God . . . but at the time, that's what I thought."

Ward said, and again she hesitated, but she said, "I guess it sounds horrid, but I'm looking forward to that experience again. It was so pleasant, so peaceful, so refreshing. I don't want to leave my family, but even if I do, I know they'll be joining me at some point.

"I have learned the importance of each day. I didn't get to look at the other side. I wonder what is beyond that door. I know it is something wonderful but I don't know what it's like. I don't think that everything is going to be like it was in the room . . . I think of it as a holding room . . . while someone decided what to do about me. I wasn't supposed to be there."

Ward has no doubt that she was dead and had she not returned, then her family would have grieved for her. She would have been as dead as the ancient Romans. But now she talks to her kids about what she saw, trying to tell them of the comfort and peace that she experienced. She wanted them to understand that death was nothing to fear. Dying might be a horrible experience, but once that was over, death itself was wonderful. The best they could hope for was a long, full life and then to die, at peace in bed.

"I think of this experience as a gift. I'm no longer afraid of death and I don't hesitate to talk to others about it. I want everyone to understand what I saw . . . I don't want to become a missionary but I would like to end some of the fear that people have. I want them to feel comfortable with the thought of death and dying."

She went on to say, however, "I think I understand why we don't understand this better. What would happen if everyone knew that after death . . . existence became a beautiful experience. Then wouldn't everyone, when faced with pain . . . loss of a loved one, loss of a job . . . any trouble in life, then wouldn't they see that the easiest course is to just check out. Why go through the pain when we can just stop living with that pain and move into another, more beautiful, more peaceful realm. We have to be careful that we don't let death become the way out of even the trivial but unpleasant events of this life.

"I learned that life is important . . . but it's not so important that we have to go through so much . . . turmoil. We have to learn that there are things more important than a job or gaining money or acquiring more than the neighbors . . . we must build our relationships with others."

Ward was quiet for a moment and then repeated, "It's the relationships that are important. We must learn to live together."

Four

William Smith

"I just knew I was going to die," said William Smith.* "I knew it from the time I woke up in the morning until it happened."

Smith, like many who had served in combat, had a premonition that he would die that day. Those who have the feeling sometimes tell friends of it. Others keep it to themselves. Once, in a great while, the prediction becomes reality and the soldier is killed.

That was what happened to Smith. According to him, it was a day just like any other for a helicopter pilot in Vietnam in the late 1960s. He had graduated from high school and had made no real plans for college. The draft loomed large, but Smith wasn't concerned about it.

"A friend . . . told me about the Army . . . their Warrant Officer Flight Program. It re-

---

*Name changed at the request of the subject.

quired a high-school diploma and you had to take some aptitude tests. I passed them and was told I could sign up for flight school. In fact, the recruiter called frequently and I began to feel like a top high-school football prospect who had a good senior year."

Smith hadn't really thought about the war in Vietnam. It was on the news nightly, but he paid no attention to it. He remembered a discussion with friends where he wasn't even aware that the Viet Cong were South Vietnamese fighting against the government in Saigon. He was more interested in sports and girls and movies . . . and girls. The politics of Vietnam didn't interest him in the least, even as it became clear that friends of his were being drafted and that they were being quickly assigned to Vietnam.

"I figured by the end of flight school, more than a year away, the war would be over . . . I would know how to fly a helicopter, a skill that few civilians could afford to learn for themselves. I envisioned a job with an airline and a future that was assured without having to spend four years in college learning the same sort of crap I had to learn in high school. Things that would do me no good once I was out of school."

Smith spent his year in flight school and then, just like everyone else in his class at Fort Rucker, he was assigned to fly helicopters in Vietnam with a three-week leave before having to report to the replacement depot in San Francisco. Smith still didn't think much about Vietnam and what it meant. Even with orders to the war, it was an abstract concept to him.

"I was going and there was nothing I could do about it . . . I had gambled and lost . . . and really didn't care much about it," said Smith.

In Vietnam, Smith was assigned to an assault helicopter company in the Three Corps tactical zone, which meant the area around Saigon and west to the Cambodia border. The terrain was urban, then rice paddy and then mountainous near Tay Ninh.

According to Smith, the missions ran the gamut from moving troops and supplies to medevac and combat assaults. Once he had his in-country orientation flight and the various check rides out of the way, he began to fly nearly every day.

"Once I got there and learned the ropes, it wasn't that bad. A daily grind, flying, which was fun . . . that sounds like a terrible thing to say since we were fighting a war . . . but the flying was good," said Smith. "I just didn't think about the people getting killed on the ground."

"I think everyone in that situation begins to think, at one time or another, he is going to die. I remember waking up and knowing that I was going to die on that day . . . I was calm though because I don't think I really believed it. It was there and if I let it come through, then I wouldn't have been able to function. Instead, I decided to be very careful but to not do anything out of the ordinary . . . it seemed that in all the movies, it was the guy who changed his routine who died. Something happened, he got scared, changed his routine and died because of it. I wasn't going to do that."

The morning missions went off quickly and easily. It was very routine. "I don't think anyone fired a shot at the flight in the morning." During the afternoon, they were working with an ARVN [South Vietnamese Army] unit. "The LZs [landing zones] were cold . . . no enemy around them. We never took the Vietnamese into a hot area first."

The flight was on final, into the LZ, a treeline to the right that wrapped around toward the front. There was a rising cloud of yellow smoke on top of a rice-paddy dike and the lead ship was heading toward it.

"I remember everything now in slow motion. I could hear the doorguns firing on full suppression . . . firing into the trees to keep the enemy heads down, if there was any enemy in there . . . There was a whine of the aircraft's turbine, the popping of the blades, and talk on the radio . . . Someone called, 'We're taking fire on the right,' . . . I was [angry] about that because he hadn't told who it was so we didn't know exactly where it was . . . Just someone shooting on the right side of the flight."

The windshield then disintegrated. "I heard the snaps as the rounds hit . . . I felt something slam into my chest, but the chicken plate [ceramic chest protector] stopped it. I couldn't breathe for a moment . . .

"There was a moment . . . just a moment, when I was confused . . . I just didn't know what was happening. Then, in an instant, I was looking down on the scene. I was outside of the aircraft, looking down on it . . . almost like I was suddenly in the C & C [command and control aircraft]."

Like Dolembo, Smith remembered no period of transition. The windshield was shattered by the bullets smashing through it. Then Smith was outside, looking down as the helicopter shuddered, spun to the left and slammed into the ground, left side low.

"The gunships were working over the treeline. I was amazed by the colors . . . they were so vivid . . . greens that hurt the eyes . . . jet black smoke . . . that sort of expanded upward toward me."

The black engulfed him, hiding the scene below him. Smith was confused by it and then noticed a light coming from it, but it seemed to be a long way off. "It was a bright light . . . pure . . . like a magnesium fire. I thought one of the aircraft was burning and that was what I was seeing."

The confusion was gone in an instant. "I don't know how to describe this . . . Someone was talking to me, quietly, calmly, telling me not to worry. I don't know where the voice was coming from. It was . . . in my head . . . and I was no longer confused, worried or scared."

The light expanded, like the fire burning brighter. Smith stared at it and was told, "Relax. Everything is going to be fine."

Smith didn't recognize the voice. "It was no one I knew . . . but it felt familiar. If I could just concentrate I thought I might remember who it was but I still don't know who was speaking to me."

Smith still hadn't moved. The bright light was now the size of a light bulb in the distance, brilliantly white, but there was no motion. He wasn't moving and he didn't think the light was moving either.

"I had questions," said Smith. "Lots of them, but I got the impression that they weren't important. I thought that if I could think of the right questions I could get the answers, but I couldn't think of them."

The light began to grow. Smith didn't know if he was moving or if the light was coming toward him. He thought that there was a tunnel, a circular area. "I was standing there . . . or maybe I was floating there, but in the black

I couldn't tell . . . All I know is that I wasn't worried or scared. I felt good, happy, almost joyous. I had the feeling that I had arrived home after the completion of my tour in Vietnam."

According to Smith, the voice kept repeating one message, one thought. "Everything is going to work out fine. Just don't worry."

"I didn't get any sort of message . . . nothing for me to share with the rest of the world . . . I just knew that everything was going to be fine . . . I wanted to move closer to the light . . . it seemed that it . . . I don't know how to say it or describe it . . . I just wanted to be near it."

Smith said that there was one thought in his mind. "I wondered if this was it."

For Smith there was no passage of time. He was just there, observing everything around him. The bright light, "hovering" in front of him and black all around him.

"I was interested in what was going to happen to me . . . The one thing I remember vividly . . . very vividly . . . was that I had no desire to learn what was happening . . . I guess you'd say, on the ground. I had been in a helicopter and then I wasn't and I wasn't concerned about that. I just wanted to join with the light and that was it."

Before that happened, Smith was overwhelmed by a sense of sadness because he knew that he didn't belong. "I was aware that it was a mistake. I wasn't supposed to be dead . . . I hadn't realized until that point that I was dead."

The light receded slightly, the glow dimming, but Smith was still aware of the voice. He knew that he had been gravely wounded and that "I was in trouble on the ground . . . I didn't want to go back to Earth if I was going to be paralyzed or lose an arm or leg . . . it was then I realized that I hadn't felt my hands or feet . . .

"I believe that there was a question asked of me. Someone wanted to know if I really wanted to return. It seemed that the decision was mine . . . somehow someone had screwed up . . . that was my impression . . . a mistake had been made."

Smith laughed. "I couldn't understand that. If what I was seeing was right, how could they make a mistake . . . but here I was, outside of the war with an option to go back."

The light was fading from him and Smith knew that he had to return. He felt there was something that he needed to do, though he didn't know what it might be. That was just an impression left with him.

The black faded, he was aware of sound all around him. Machine guns were firing, hammering, and he could smell the JP-4 jet fuel as it leaked out of the ruptured fuel cells of the badly damaged helicopter. Someone was shouting and hands were fumbling with the seatbelt around him. "My head hurt and there was a tingling in my hands and feet. It hurt to breathe."

Someone was looking at him through the shattered remains of the windshield. Someone else was in the door, trying to drag him clear. He was aware of a strong copper odor and knew that it was blood. He tried to see his co-pilot but the doorgunner was crouched over the radio console, turned toward him. "He was talking but I couldn't hear what he was saying. I didn't care either."

He didn't remember anything after that one brief instant. He knew he had to get out of the helicopter but couldn't move. The next thing he remembered was that it was cool and there was pain in his head and chest. It was dark again, and there was a point of light, but it was a dull electric bulb. He knew exactly where he was. Inside the air-conditioned quonset huts that made up one of the evac hospitals.

"I looked down . . . I remembered seeing one of those movies where there was a big tent in the sheets because they had cut off some-one's leg, but there was no tent . . . and both my hands were outside the sheet."

Although there was some pain and his head still ached, Smith was relaxed and calm. He knew that he would get better. He'd been told that everything would be all right while he had been in the light.

And then he remembered that wounded soldiers didn't stay long in Vietnam. They were evacuated as soon as it was medically feasible for it. He would be out of Vietnam in a matter of hours and probably sent home for rest.

The experience changed his attitudes toward life and death. As he lay in the hospital bed, he had a chance to think about what happened. He didn't know what it had been, but he was sure that he had been killed in the helicopter. There were no doctors to make the pronouncement, but he knew. He had died there, of his wounds, seen the other side and then chosen to return, or rather, been forced to return.

"I can't explain it . . . I knew that I had to come back whether I wanted to or not. I have something to do . . . but I don't know what . . . I have a sense of purpose that I never had before. I had been drifting through life letting things come at me with no direction."

Smith said that he had never thought about being a pilot until his friend told him the Army was accepting high school grads for flight school. He hadn't bothered to send out letters to various colleges because he just hadn't thought about it. He drifted through high school, taking the path of least resistance. That was now gone. Smith wasn't going to drift along through his life.

"I stopped making the easy decisions, but made the hard ones. I stopped letting others set up situations so that I had little or no real choice . . . I guess you could say that I allowed the situations to develop until there wasn't much that could be done. Drifting is the perfect word for it. Take no responsibility, just slide along.

He also said that "I knew that things would be okay for me. I was badly wounded, but I would get better and there would be no residual problems. I think of some of the guys with arms and legs shot off and realize how lucky I was. We took a bunch of hits through the cockpit. The co-pilot was hit in the knee and it messed him up. Sort of locked his knee on him. I was hit badly, but I knew I'd get better."

Back in the United States, it was determined that his wounds were bad enough that he could be discharged with a partial disability. There was therapy he had to undergo because of the wounds, but he eventually regained full use of both arms. He was in therapy for several months, first at an Army hospital close to his home of record and later in a private hospital on an out-patient basis.

"Some Vietnam vets talk about bad dreams and flashbacks, but I don't have those. It's like . . . I'm at peace with the whole situation . . . I mean, I just flew helicopters and I didn't kill anyone while doing it . . . I was in the thick of it more than once, but I was just doing my job. The Army taught me to fly, and I flew. When the bullets started flying, I ignored them and concentrated on what I had to do. I was the pilot, I had to get the aircraft down, and then back up. Keep the grunts from getting overrun by getting them out."

Smith believed that his experience provided him with a perspective that most Vietnam veterans don't have. "They look on the hardships . . . the sacrifice . . . that no one cared about. Friends died and the outcome was the one the politicians determined. What happened on the battlefield made no difference. Some of them can't handle that . . . I know that it was something that we all had to go through . . . It's hard to describe . . . maybe it was like a giant test. We're all tested and part of mine was the trip across the pond [Pacific Ocean] . . . it was something that I had to do to grow into the person I am."

To Smith, his near-death experience was a learning situation. He saw what it was like on the other side and he learned that what happened here, while important, was not as important as how he treated others. He needed to be more aware of them as people and not as props put out for his convenience and to populate his world.

"That was the revelation I had . . . I know that some people talk about great and profound thoughts. All I realized was that other people had feelings like me. I guess I realized that what makes me mad makes others mad but that I shouldn't let it. None of it's important."

Like many of the others, Smith said that he was no longer afraid of death. He was clear on that point. He knew what it was like and he was looking forward to it. Maybe not exactly looking forward to it, but waiting in anticipation because he would have the opportunity to see what was beyond the light. Death was nothing more than a change in environment. Life, according to him, is sort of a transition. What was beyond the light was something to look forward to.

"I don't know exactly what is over there because I didn't get to see much of it. Just a hint of it. A bright light filled with love that wanted me to be comfortable. I worry about how I'm going to die because there are many horrible ways to die . . . cancer, AIDS, traffic accidents or murder . . . some of those things can drag out in horrible ways. But once that process is over, then it is something good and clean and wonderful."

Smith was sure that he had been dead . . ."Or as close to it as you can get." But there was no one around who could make that pronouncement. It is a feeling that Smith has, based on what he saw.

"I think," said Smith, "I was standing at the gate. Had I made another decision, I wouldn't have to ask the questions because I would know. But there was something there . . . something that suggested to me that I had to return . . . I have this feeling of a mission . . . of a purpose. Because of that, I made my choice to return . . . I now think of it as a choice to return and I don't regret it. At that time it was the right thing for me to do."

Five

Judy Thomas

Judy Thomas had thought it was nothing worse than a lingering cold. She had a cough, sneezes and a fever. Her eyes hurt and her chest ached, but she believed that a day or two in bed would be the best, so she called her boss and told him, called her mother and told her, and then, with the vaporizer bubbling, she climbed into bed.

She turned on the TV to watch the afternoon movies on cable, not really caring about the plot or the characters but glad to have the comforting background noise of people talking about trivia. She dozed, woke, hot and sweaty, thinking that she wanted to get something to drink but without the energy to get out of bed. She'd kicked the covers off but was still hot and miserable.

Reaching for the phone to call her mother, she passed out. Regaining consciousness a moment later, she knew that she was very sick. It was not just a bad cold.

Now she was scared. "I knew that I had to get up. I had to get some help but I was too sick to move. I just couldn't move even when I knew how important it was. I wanted someone to come to help but I couldn't get up the energy to call them."

She tried to reach the phone, knocked it from the nightstand, and wanted to cry in frustration. She couldn't reach it on the floor and didn't seem to have the strength to get out of bed.

"At that moment, I knew that I would die if I didn't get some help but I didn't move."

She awoke again but it was dark. She could hear the TV in the background. She looked at the window and was surprised by the bright square of light there. She stared at it, wondering what it was. "I couldn't figure it out because it was night but the window was so very bright . . . like a searchlight playing through it."

The phone on the floor was forgotten. She sat up. "I was amazed . . . before, I could barely lift my hand, now I was feeling fine . . . not hot or cold or sick . . ."

She stood up to walk to the window to see what is going on outside. As she turned to look back at the TV, she saw something in her bed. "I thought the covers were all bunched up, but

then I saw hair. I was confused by that. Someone was in my bed and I couldn't figure out
how that could be."

She felt the light on her back, glowing and
warm. "I was at peace, feeling . . . good. I was
happy and calm, even with someone in my
bed . . . Then I realized that it was me. I was
still in bed even though I was standing there
near the window, looking back at myself."

Her confusion didn't last long. It was replaced by a "sense of wonder." She was amazed
by everything that was going on around her.
The light seemed to be getting brighter all the
time. The image on the TV screen faded,
washed out by the brightness of the light.

"It was strange," Thomas said. "There
didn't seem to be any shadows. The light was
at the window, glowing through it, but there
were no shadows anywhere . . . not on the bed
or on the floor or on the walls. It was a brilliantly bright light behind me but it seemed to
come from everywhere at once . . . it's impossible for me to describe.

"I turned and looked at the window. It was
moving away from me until it looked as if I
was staring down a long tunnel at a light at
the far end . . . my room was gone and I don't
know where I was."

There was no sensation of motion. The light
was growing and she believed that she was moving toward it rather than it coming at her. "Ev-

erything had faded away . . . I wanted to get closer to that light . . . there was something there that I wanted to get closer to . . ."

She didn't reach the light. It expanded outward until there was no darkness around her. Now she was in a field with a fence at the far end. A riot of wildflowers carpeted the meadow. The sky overhead was a deep, bright blue with not a cloud in it.

"I was at the far end [of the meadow] and knew that I had to get to the fence at the other end . . . I couldn't see a gate and there was a line of trees behind the fence . . . there was no break in it either."

She began to walk forward, filled with hope and joy and feeling calm. She just knew that all she had to do was cross the meadow. That was a destination that would give her complete and total joy.

Near the fence she could see a figure standing. It seemed to be surrounded by a golden glow. "I didn't recognize it but I believed it was someone holy. Maybe Jesus or maybe God, but I knew that when I got there, everything would be solved. I would know who it was.

"I don't know how I knew that . . . that the person was holy . . . I was still confused and my mind was filled with questions . . . then, suddenly, they were all answered. I knew what was happening to me . . . I had died in my bed, at home and all alone, but I didn't care . . . nothing on Earth mattered anymore. I wasn't a part of it anymore."

She knew that all she had to do was reach the fence. Paradise was on the other side of the fence. "I kept on walking and as I did, I could hear a voice in my head telling me that everything was going to be fine. Nothing mattered now. Everything I wanted to know would be told to me shortly . . . The voice promised answers."

More figures joined the first. "When I saw them, I recognized some of them. I saw my sister who had died at seven . . . She was full grown now, but I recognized her anyway. I was so happy that I felt like crying . . . and my grandpa was there. He had been my favorite . . . and now I was going to see him again . . . all I had to do was walk across the field . . . The funny thing is that I didn't feel like running to see them. I was filled with joy but there was no desire to run. I was suddenly much more patient than I had ever been."

As she neared her destination, the brightness of everything began to fade. "The wildflowers weren't quite as colorful, the grass not quite as green and the sky not nearly so blue. The bright, golden light was gone and I couldn't see my sister any more."

Thomas said that she was suddenly sad because she knew that a mistake had been made. "No one said anything but I knew that I didn't belong . . . I was going to have to go back . . . I have heard since this that others are given a choice but I didn't have one.

"I wanted to talk to my sister before I returned. I really wanted to know what she had been doing all these years . . . There are many times that I still miss her . . . but now I think of her as on a trip overseas where she can't return easily . . . I miss her and wish that she would come home but I know that I'll be seeing her again someday."

The scene then "winked" out. Suddenly it was dark again and she opened her eyes. There was a dull light on somewhere and she rolled her head to one side. Her mother was sitting beside her and she was in the hospital. Equipment was hooked up to her, monitoring her body functions, the heart monitor beeping quietly.

"When I opened my eyes, my mom grabbed my hand and broke down crying. She thought that she had lost me. She thought that I was going to die."

Thomas said that her mother had tried to call her a number of times during that day but kept getting a busy signal. She knew her daughter was ill, at home, and was getting worried about her. "I sometimes take the phone off the hook," said Thomas, "and my mom knew that. But it had been busy for such a long time that she got scared. She came over, couldn't see any lights on inside and used the key to get in. She found me lying in my bed unconscious. She called for an ambulance to take me to the hospital.

"I don't know if I was ever dead. There was no one around to take my pulse or listen to my heartbeat. I think I was dead . . . I know that I saw what happens after you die."

The doctors told her that she had been very sick and that it had been close several times. They were sure that she was going to die and that there was nothing they could do to stop it. She had been too sick to do much when they had finally gotten her to the hospital.

However, no one could say whether or not she had died in the clinical sense. When she arrived at the hospital, her vital signs were almost nonexistent, but there was blood pressure, there was respiration and there was a heartbeat. Because of that, the consensus was that she hadn't actually died but she had been about as close as she could get and still recover. Had she not been taken to the hospital when she was, she certainly would have died.

She said, "Maybe I had died briefly and then came back. I believe, in my own mind, that is what happened. But it wasn't my time to die for whatever reason and I came back."

Like so many others, her views of life and death changed radically. "Up to this point I really hadn't thought about death all that much. It was just something that happened to everyone at sometime . . . no one gets out of life alive as they say . . . I didn't think about it, preferring to live my life without worrying about something I could do nothing about. Besides, I think I was thinking that I would be the only immortal on the planet. I would live forever even if everyone else died . . . but now . . . I don't want to say that I'm looking forward to it . . . but I am, in a way because I'll have a chance to see my sister again."

That was the only thing that she regretted about the experience. "It was such a wonderful thing . . . I just can't tell you how good and wonderful it was . . . I was at such peace. I had been hurting before. The coughing was terrible and my whole body hurt when I coughed. I had a headache but didn't have the energy to get anything for it . . . I could just lay in bed hoping to sleep and wishing that I felt better . . . Then, suddenly, I did. I felt great. No pain . . . no cold, nothing. I was healthy again with no after-effects.

"When I saw my sister, I recognized her immediately. I knew it was her and I was filled with joy. I couldn't wait to tell her how much I missed her . . . I have the feeling that she knew it, too, and that she wanted to talk to me . . . we just didn't have the chance to share anything. I knew that we would later, years later for me . . . I got the impression from somewhere that it wouldn't be so long for her . . .

"That reminds me . . . I had no sense of time. I don't know how long I was there . . . I know that sounds strange. I should say, Well, it seems to have lasted thirty minutes or an hour, but I have no sense of the time at all. I was walking across the field and I guess you could say time was passing because I was moving but I just have no sense of it."

It was because she saw her sister that she "is looking forward" to another reunion. She knows, for that to happen, she must die first, but that prospect holds no fear for her. "I know that when I die I'll still be me. I'll live beyond that event and that I'll be with friends and family I haven't seen since they died. We'll all have a chance to talk."

Because of that, she no longer fears the prospect of death. "If there was one thing I could tell people, it's that they have nothing to worry about. It's a beautiful, wonderful experience. It's just one more aspect of life."

Thomas doesn't think of what she learned as anything overly profound. What she talks about is simple matters and everyday living. "I know that most of what we consider important isn't really. We all get angry when the dummies sit in front of us at red lights and don't move when they change to green . . . or they cut us off in traffic . . . or commit some other, minor outrage. We just shouldn't get upset by it . . . none of that is important. We've all lost sight of what's really important and that is how we treat one another."

"Walking across the meadow, I felt so warm and happy and at peace. I was filled with love . . . I just can't explain it . . . I can't tell you what it was like. I seemed to shed my beliefs and there was Jesus waiting for me. I've never been particularly religious but I knew who it was . . . there was just no question about it."

But that didn't change her habits. Thomas still doesn't attend church. "That's not necessary. Churches are good for what they do . . . provide help and comfort to those who need it . . . but I don't have to go there to know God or Jesus. It doesn't make you a good person to go to church once a week if you are unkind and hateful the rest. Putting on a good face doesn't really fool anyone anyway.

"I don't think God is there, at the church, with a list, checking to see who is in church and who isn't. The sense I got was that he is more interested in how we treat one another. Do you do kind deeds even when no one is looking to see it? Or do you just pay lip service to this . . ."

Thomas said, "I have no real regrets about being sent back, because I'll return to the meadow. But it's good for my mom. I didn't want to leave her alone. She needs someone. She's had a hard life."

Thomas said, "The one thing I do regret, I guess, is that I can't convince people about any of this. They just don't want to hear it. Maybe it's because they think I'm somehow denying their religion or their beliefs. I don't think that it means that Christ didn't live or that he isn't the Son of God. There is nothing that I saw that could lead to that conclusion.

Or maybe they just don't want to talk about it . . . to talk about death and dying. But it was all so beautiful and wonderful and peaceful. There is nothing for them to worry about. There is nothing to be concerned about. It is just one more aspect of living.

"I'm looking forward to it . . . maybe not dying because that wasn't pleasant. I was very sick. I was miserable and thought that I wanted to die never expecting it to happen. But now I know the truth, I can't wait . . . No, I'm not planning to do anything to cut my life short. I will live it the best I can, and then, when it is over naturally, I will return and meet my sister again. That will be a beautiful situation."

Six

The Death Dream

Everyone has had a death dream at some time during his or her life. It might be falling out a window, off a cliff, or being killed by criminals, enemy soldiers, friends, or mysterious strangers. Such dreams are frightening, sometimes preventing the victim from sleeping again for the night, or the next several days. Often they are frequently repeated, making it even harder to sleep the rest of the night.

In my own case, it was in a passenger car with three other people. I was in the back seat of a large, four-door passenger car. We drove off a cliff in a fog, unable to see the road, or the ground around it. For a moment, I was relaxed, and then I realized that we hadn't hit the ground. I knew the coming crash would be fatal because we had been airborne too long. And then I woke up.

A friend, for some strange reason, dreamed he was working as a dishwasher in New York

City. The criminal, his killer, burst through the double, stainless steel, barroom-type doors, grabbed him and threw him up against the wall. With a knife, he cut my friend's throat. He knew he was going to die because he was bleeding badly from the wound. And then he woke.

He was unable to sleep the rest of the night. In fact, he had trouble sleeping for the rest of the week and month, even though he was not a dishwasher and did not live in New York City. He had no plans to move or to change his occupation to fit the circumstances of the dream.

Police officers and soldiers often dream they are in a fire fight, close to being killed by the criminals or the enemy. They have their weapons, and they fire them. Sometimes they can't seem to hit a target, even when the target is only four or five feet away. Or, they can see the rounds striking the enemy's body, but the bullets have no effect. The enemy keeps coming. And then they wake up.

In a few cases, they don't wake up before they die. One man told his family and friends that he dreamed he was in Nicaragua, married, and on some kind of duty. He didn't understand why he was in Nicaragua, who he was married to, or exactly what his duty was. These were the points that were vivid to him in the context of the dream.

For some reason, he was shot in the chest.

He felt the round hitting and knew that he was going to die. He didn't know why he was shot, only that he was. Before he woke up, he died in the dream.

That seemed to be a change from the conventional wisdom that you never die in your dreams. A dozen questions sprang to my mind, such as: After you died in a dream, did you awaken or did you dream of what happened next? Did everything fade to black like the ending of a movie or was there something more? Could you remember anything about that aspect of the dream after you awakened?

But I never got to ask the questions because, when I asked to speak to the young man, I learned that he was dead. He'd gone to Nicaragua, married, and was shot in the chest. The wound was fatal.

There are other types of death dreams and these parallel the near-death experience. Melody Anderson was the first to mention it to me. It was something that sounded interesting but not completely relevant to the near-death experience.

Anderson, as a young girl, dreamed that she was in a bright, white room. Everything in it was white. She was in a white bed, in the white room with white walls and a white ceiling. There was virtually no color around her, with the exception of a small window. The only hint of color was behind the window. A beautiful

golden glow that appeared to look like a star
that was coming closer to the window. Anderson knew that she wasn't moving toward it. It
was moving toward her. "It just expanded as I
saw it coming towards me—I was just ecstatic
and I said, 'He's here.'"

She knew that she was going to die. "I knew
without a doubt that it was my moment to
die . . . and that . . . was going to be my transition point."

But she wasn't frightened by the revelation
because of the golden glow. She was at peace . . .
"totally at peace . . . the gold light comes toward the room and it just gets bigger and bigger . . . and as it gets to the window, I'm just
smiling . . . I'm so happy, peacefully happy."

Anderson knew that everything was going to
be fine. The gold light filled the white room
and she knew that nothing bad would happen
to her once the light entered the room. "The
light . . . until all of the sudden it just stepped
into the room and it just totally filled the room.

"I was in ecstasy . . . and then I woke up."

But the blissful feeling didn't desert her
when she awakened. "I was blissful . . ."

But waking up didn't upset her. There was
no doubt that what she had experienced was a
dream, but in that moment, she said, "I knew
that . . . death was nothing to fear." It totally
changed her outlook on life and death.

"It translated to endings," she said. "Relationships could end or that friends and family could die and it just brought to me a total assurance that it always . . . that there is something more than what we're aware."

Anderson has spoken to many others who have had a near-death experience, and the question that had to be asked was if this, the death dream, paralleled the near-death experience. She said, "I would hear about the light and even though mine doesn't correspond . . . I didn't travel, the light came to me and that seemed to be different . . . there weren't any people. It was not about people at all, but the feeling was there . . . there was the golden lighted presence . . . to me made it very similar. It appears that from talking to other people that it has had a similar beneficial impact on my life. In that way it's very similar . . . It changed my whole outlook on death and life and beginnings and endings."

Psychologist Paula Land, who practices in Ruidoso, New Mexico, also had what could be considered a death dream that parallels the near-death phenomenon. It suggests some things to researchers, and provides some interesting insights to those who have them.

According to Land, her dream began with her walking into the living room. The drawers and the cabinets were slowly opening and closing. She stood watching for a moment and then asked, not in the brave voice she wanted, but in a scared, squeaky voice, "Is this a spirit?"

In response, a drawer opened and closed. "I guess you could say that that was my answer."

She demanded that any energy that was not the white light of God, leave the room. "At that point, the scene switched and I was with several of my family members and some close friends."

She continued, "We were sort of swooped up, taken up in a white room into a structure like a light house. There was a white glowing light shining in . . . We were allowed to experience, without using different senses, the clouds, the sky, the heavens . . . God had no physical form in my dream. [I'm] not even sure there was an actual voice . . . more like a telepathic kind of knowing but there was absolute certainty that the energy communicating was 'the God energy.' "

Land was told that God was going to open up heaven to allow them to experience heaven. "We were allowed to experience what it was like to be on the other side of life and it was absolute bliss . . ."

The assembled people were told, according to Land's dream, that they had two choices. They could enter into heaven formless or they could chose to bring heaven to form. One by one they dived into a pool of water that looked like the baptistery in a church. One would dive in and there would be silence. Then another would dive and there would be silence.

Land said, "Finally I was the only one left and I sort of scooted back the bubbles on top of the water to look underneath to see what had actually happened . . . Sure enough, their physical bodies were under there. They looked . . . beautifully happy and peaceful . . . finally it's my turn."

But, before she could make her dive, a strong force stopped her and pushed her back. Something said, "Now wait. Stop." She was told, "You can't go."

She was crushed and wanted to know why. She was told, "You've made an agreement. Your job is to stay and help bring heaven into form and to help the world to understand . . ."

When she returned to Earth, she was required to tell the family and friends of those who had elected to stay that their loved ones were gone. She felt deep sorrow for the loss, but was happy for their freedom.

"I was trying to explain to the others what heaven had felt like, what bliss was like."

And then she woke up.

"I will never forget this as long as I live. First . . . I reached out to see if my dog was there . . . then I noticed that my nightgown was drenched . . . my heart was pounding . . . it was absolutely the most profound dream I have ever had in my life."

Land, in her work as a psychologist, has spoken to many patients who have had near-death experiences. She mentioned an older woman, who related her "death" when she was struck by an eighteen-wheeler. The woman related that she had experienced many of the elements of the near-death experience, but she recovered from her injuries. The woman, when this happened in the 1950s, had never heard of the near-death experience. In fact, until she related the story to Land, she had no idea that anyone else had ever had a similar experience. She was delighted to learn of others.

Asked if the death-dream experience related to the near-death experience, Land said, "I think, in my dream, there was more emotion . . . They don't experience the terror . . . they probably do experience the bliss and the peace . . . but in my dream there were the real ups and downs. There was bliss, there was sorrow, there was fear . . . excitement. If you could have interviewed one of those people who decided to go into heaven formless, they probably would have described [something] more like a near-death experience."

Land believed that the dream had opened up new levels of consciousness for her and in that respect it was like the near-death experience. It changed her attitude toward death and allowed her to speak more freely to her patients about death. In the past, she "would dance" around the questions, using the euphemisms when she talked about death and dying. Now she is more blunt and wonders if that doesn't make it easier on her patients to speak to her about their thoughts of death and dying.

The question then becomes, is the near-death experience a true glimpse of the other side or a psychological manifestation of something else? Land, of course, hadn't experienced near death, but a dream that related to the near-death phenomenon. However, in the course of her work as a psychologist, she had spoken to many others who had experienced near death. Her observations would be interesting, I thought.

But the answer was less than clear. She said, "I think it's sort of one in the same. Do I think they (those who claim near-death experiences) glimpse the other side? Yes."

The near-death experiences are not hallucinations, according to Dr. Land. It is her opinion that something takes place. To describe it as a physical event is difficult because the physical body does not participate. As Moody said, one criterion for a near-death experience is an out-of-body experience. The near-death experience might be a "real" event, but it is not a physical event.

It is a problem to design a "scientific" test to measure the near-death experience. The NDE rarely happen at a convenient time or place. Usually there is a traumatic event. Doctors and nurses, sometimes with complex medical equipment, are present, but they are concerned with saving a life and not observing, in any dispassionate way, what is happening to the subject. Any measurements or observations that might be of some use are lost in the turmoil.

But even if it was possible, during the near-death experience, to make readings of instruments, or to observe the subject in a laboratory setting, it is almost impossible to design an experiment that could explain the phenomenon, or that would duplicate it.

Hollywood did come up with an experiment that was shown in *Flatliners*. The experiments proceeded with the assumption that the near-death experience could be recreated at the whim of medical students or fledgling doctors. To experience near-death, it is necessary to "kill" the patient and then work to resuscitate him or her. That was the basis for the Hollywood version.

But, according to many doctors, there are thousands of people who have come very close to death. They have clinically died and report no near-death experience. People who have drowned, who have been underwater for fifteen or twenty minutes and later resuscitated, saw nothing while unconscious or after they had "died."

The near-death experience, then, is "selective." Not everyone who is in a nearly fatal traffic accident, or who has a heart attack, or who nearly dies on the operating table, reports a near-death experience.

That doesn't mean they haven't experienced something similar. It is that they have no memory of it. Or maybe they never reached the point where they entered the tunnel and saw the light.

There are, literally, dozens of reasons why some people in very traumatic circumstances report an NDE and others do not. The answers could be simple or they could be almost impossibly complex. The only real answer now is that we simply don't know enough to explain it.

Land said that her patient who had never heard of the near-death experience even though she herself had experienced one, hadn't been contaminated by any of these outside influences. She hadn't read about others and therefore her perceptions, as reported, were unclouded by the influence of those other reports. It was interesting that her near-death experience paralleled, in many respects, the NDEs of others.

Of course, as Land was quick to point out, scientifically, that means very little. There is the possibility that the near-death experience, if it is a psychological manifestation, could produce similar observations in various patients. That is why, according to Land, "other psychologists in the health-care field can say, 'Well, you can't prove it.' "

Anderson felt that her death dream, because of the circumstances, was a close parallel to the near-death experience. The light wasn't bright white, but golden, and she felt completely at peace, just as those who have NDEs claim. It was a blissful, wonderful event. In the context of the dream she knew that she was going to die, but the prospect didn't frighten her. She was prepared.

Land, though she classifies it as a death dream, and believed that she was allowed a glimpse of heaven, did not die in her dream. She believes, in the dream, that she had died, but there was no process of dying, just the sudden transition from life to a state of death.

But both of them related that the death dream had changed their perceptions of life and death and had an effect on their lives. Anderson, of course, as a practitioner of past-life regression, is more inclined to accept testimony of the near-death experience. That is not to say that her observations are less valid than others.

Does the death dream suggest that the near-death experience is a psychological problem? Not at all. There are alternative explanations. The parallel seen between the death dream and near-death might be nothing more than the result of contamination. Both Land and Anderson were aware of the near-death phenomenon. They may have related their dreams to NDE because of that prior knowledge.

Of course, there are major differences between the death dream and NDEs. Those might also be significant. Or, it could be that the death dream allows us a glimpse of the "other side" without the trauma of having to die in some sort of fatal accident or to have a life threatening illness.

While the death dream is clearly the mind at work, it might be at work on a level that is not available to us in a conscious state. The death dream might tap into a higher level of consciousness so that it provides us with a true glimpse of something that we can't see while conscious.

But the near-death experience might have nothing to do with the operation of the human mind. It might be a glimpse of the reality that exists on the other side.

Dr. Land doesn't believe that the near-death phenomenon is psychological. She believes that it is a true experience. She believes that the death dream provides information on one level, and that the NDE provides it on another. The real point is, that both are very real to those who have experienced them.

Part II:
Near-Death Experience
and . . .

Seven

Near-Death Tales of Terror

Almost universally, the near-death experience is something pleasant, overwhelming in its beauty, and profound in its effect on each life. Nearly everyone reports an uplifting experience of such magnitude that it is impossible to speak to them without sensing their feelings of awe and wonder. Each person believes his or her experience is based in reality, though not necessarily in the reality that we all experience on a daily basis.

There are, however, those who have not had pleasant experiences after death. The near-death experience has profoundly affected their outlook but not as pleasantly or beautifully as it has for the vast majority of the people.

Many of these people report that a near-death experience has had a disruptive effect on their lives. Their concepts of love and death and relationships are profoundly changed. While in some cases this might not be a positive benefit, the experience itself remains one filled with beauty and grace. What has happened afterwards, on this side, is the result of others who "have not seen the light." The negative reaction comes, in such cases, from a skeptical world where everything must be proved a dozen times before it is accepted and even then there are those who will never change their minds. But that is as it should be. We should demand as much proof as can be found. There is nothing wrong with skeptics demanding something more tangible than the testimony of those who have NDEs. Although there is little in the way of objective proof, there is some, and it should be examined.

But that controversy is a side effect of the near-death experience and not caused by it. There are those, however, who say that their near-death experiences were horrible and frightening. This is not the result of skepticism, but a result of the experience itself.

One woman claimed that she had been horrified by her near-death experience. She had attempted suicide, taking a bottle of pills. Found by friends, she was rushed to the hospital for emergency treatment. While there, she claimed that she had a near-death experience.

Demons, dark creatures, like those represented in the hit movie *Ghost* seemed to grow up, out of the floor. They were standing around her bed, babbling at her and trying to drag her down with them. They circled her, oblivious to the activity of the doctors and nurses working desperately to save her life. She knew they were trying to take her soul and she knew she was going to hell.

She told the doctor about the demons, but he said that she was hallucinating. There had been no demons trying to take her to hell but she was convinced they had been there.

Her experience is not like the others. She was fully conscious when she saw the demons. She did not see a tunnel, a bright light or have an out-of-body experience. And, she had taken a large number of pills that could easily have induced the hallucinations the doctor diagnosed.

The woman believes she had a near-death experience but the question that must be addressed is how was that possible? In every other case, those reporting NDE are unconscious and in some cases are dead, clinically dead. Raymond Moody, in *The Light Beyond* reports cases where there is no detectable brain activity. Because of the circumstances of the near-death experience, often the "victim" is hooked to various monitoring machines.

Moody reports that in some cases the EEG, which monitors electrical activity in the brain, has been showing a flatline. A flatline means the brain is incapable of thought or action. One of the accepted definitions of death is a lack of electrical activity in the brain.

So, by all acceptable standards, the woman who saw the demons did not have a near-death experience. Regardless of what she says, regardless of what she believes, her experience was probably induced by the drugs she had taken. It was not induced by death.

But there are others who also suggest that the near-death experience was not pleasant. One researcher, Dr. Nsama Mumbwe of the University of Zambia examined Africans who had experienced NDE. Half of them interpreted the experience as something evil and believed that they had been somehow bewitched. One thought of it as a bad omen.

That does not necessarily translate into a "bad" experience or one of fright. It does demonstrate the cultural bias of those who have near-death experiences. In fact, in *Bright Lights, Big Mystery* James Mauro reports on the cultural influence on NDE. Although descriptions vary from culture to culture, it might be that the people must "borrow images from personal experience." The variations are a result, not of differing experiences but of different cultural elements.

Still, there are those who clearly have not had a pleasant near-death experience. They are left with fear. Aside from the case of the woman who saw the demons, we can still find people who wished their NDE had never happened.

Some of the people who have near-death experiences claim that it was terrifying although it resembles those blissful experiences reported by the vast majority of people. They approach the tunnel, see the light, but feel sucked into it, losing control of the situation. Nancy Evans Bush reported that it was as if one was looking into the gates of hell and was powerless to stop one's progress into the light.

One woman claimed that she felt at peace at first. She saw a point of light in front of her that was growing larger. She suddenly had the feeling that she was being dragged into the light and she wasn't sure that she wanted to go. She wanted to fight it.

All the time, there was a loud ringing. She was trying to concentrate but the bell kept intruding. It hurt her ears . . . or rather she later reported that she had an unpleasant sensation in her head that she associated with the ringing bell. She just wanted it to stop.

The light became bigger and brighter. No longer was she sure that she was moving toward it because she had no sensation of motion. But it was getting bigger and bigger and she felt that she was going to be overwhelmed by it, that somehow it was going to take possession of her.

Before she was "sucked" in, the light vanished and she awakened in the hospital. She told no one about the experience at that time, fearing that putting it into words would underscore the reality of the situation.

It did change her concept of life after death. What she fears now is a loss of her personal identity, though she admits that she was fully aware of herself as a single individual even as the light came toward her. She admits that she has no reason to suspect she would lose her feeling of self if she entered the light.

That is one of the major complaints by those frightened by the experience. A man—who doesn't want his name associated with the near-death experience—said that he felt no feelings of peace or calm, but experienced fright as the he watched a light coming toward him. He thought it was going to overwhelm him, taking him in even though he had no desire to enter. He wanted it to stay away from him.

He did believe that he heard a voice, but the message was garbled and he couldn't understand it. He was confused by all that was happening. He thought that he had died but wasn't sure. He didn't know how he had gotten to the point where he could see the bright light, but he knew that he didn't want to be there. Something was wrong.

That might be the key to his experience. He was confused and frightened and there was no one there to guide him farther. He was alone, trying to figure out the situation.

As the light began to fade and the voice disappeared, he felt a sense of relief. Moments later, he regained consciousness. There was pain in both his legs and he knew that he had fallen off the roof. But his sense of relief was so great that he almost didn't notice the pain.

Others report that they have been lost in a great "cosmic void." There is nothing to see or do and there is no one around them. One man said that it was his concept of hell. Absolute nothingness for all of eternity. He was just floating in the blackness around him.

By contrast, Chet Szeliga (mentioned earlier) had a near-death experience as a teenager, and found himself drifting in space above the Earth. But it wasn't just a cosmic blackness. He could look down on the Earth, seeing the clouds, continents and oceans on it as if he were standing on the moon or in orbit round the planet. His short-lived experience did not frighten him but left him with a sense of wonder about what else would happen after death.

This might be explainable by the mind set of those having these sorts of experiences. One man, seeing the blackness around him, is frightened by it because there is no explanation for it. Another, Szeliga, is in a similar environment but hasn't lost his sense of wonder. He is "blown away" by the experience and not frightened by it.

However, most of those who experience the cosmic void are devastated by it. They have a feeling that they have been abandoned and that leads to long-term despair after they return to this life.

There is a third, very small group, who believe they do see into hell. Though it is not the classical vision of hell, they do see people being tortured and tormented by others. The experience is filled with noise, a loud rushing of air that could be interpreted as the screams of those being tortured. It is an ongoing sound.

For that small group, the glimpse of the other side fills them with dread. They know that the soul survives, but they have seen something that does not fill them with peace.

It would seem that the majority of the people in the group who have unpleasant experiences have interpreted the experience negatively. They do report the tunnel, the noises claimed by many others, and even the bright light. But there is something about them that prevents them from looking on this as a positive experience.

It could be that they don't fully understand the situation. For some reason there is a vital bit of information that is not provided to them. They are alone in the tunnel, facing the light, and feeling only terror and dread. There is no welcoming presence nor family member to escort them. If it is possible, it would seem that someone didn't get the proper word so that the newly dead individual is left, for a short time, alone. Without the other aspects of the NDE, such as a welcoming committee, the person has a frightening experience.

In fact, it has been found that East Indians often report heaven as a giant bureaucracy. They have been taken because of some kind of clerical mistake and are being sent back because of it.

By taking that belief a step further, it could be said that those who find themselves alone, are alone because of a "clerical error." Somehow, someone doesn't get into the right place at the right time and therefore the person had no idea of what is happening.

There are those, however, who even on finding themselves alone do not experience fear. They have no escort or guide but are overwhelmed by feelings of wonderment, peace and love. One man found himself in a large, beautiful, sunlit meadow walking toward a fence at the base of a treeline. He kept walking, wanting to see what was on the other side of the trees, unconcerned about how he got there or about any of the other circumstances surrounding the event.

Although he was alone in a large empty field with no one there to greet him, he saw the experience as something wonderful, and although he was "jerked" back into this world, he wasn't at all frightened.

In examining the many near-death stories, one concludes that those who have bad experiences are those who choose to see them in a bad light. The elements that make the experience unpleasant are also found in those positive experiences. It is the "spin" put on the experience by those living it that makes the difference.

The exception is those who claim to have seen into hell. There is no way to find the positive spin, except to point out that they have seen that life survives death. And maybe, having looked into hell, they can change their ways in this life and avoid spending eternity there.

One man, interviewed on national TV, reported that his observations after he "died" had changed his life. Instead of staying on his criminal path, he had become an ordained minister. His glimpse of hell taught him that there was a reason to follow the path of good while on Earth.

There is no easy explanation for any of these experiences. They are frightening and as real as those of peace, calm and joy. But there are very few of them. So few that it is tempting to dismiss them as unimportant and consider them aberrant. The serious investigator cannot afford to do that.

With so little known about the NDE, *all* information about the phenomenon is important. We must, however, put the data into some perspective. We must consider the big picture. For example, we know little about the backgrounds of those who claim unpleasant experiences. Such personal histories might explain the differences just as cultural experience explains the differences in the way the situation is described.

Should we be concerned about the data that describes a darker side of the near-death experience? Not until we understand all there is to know about the factors that contribute to it. Not until there are studies that provide a hint about the background of those having the experiences.

Psychologist Kenneth Ring, who wrote *The Omega Project* suggested that there are personalities that are prone to having these sorts of experiences. According to Ring, people who were abused in childhood have a greater tendency to report near-death experiences. According to Ring, they have learned to "disassociate" which means they can "remove" themselves from the environment by seeming to separate themselves mentally from the body of the child being abused.

Ring said, "The ability to disassociate makes you more receptive to alternative realities." This means that they have learned to have "out of body" experiences which is one of the keys to the NDE.

Barbara Harris who claimed two NDEs also says that she was abused as a child. The question becomes, was Harris disassociating herself from the trauma of dying as she had during the abuse, or was she seeing something real?

And a second question that must be addressed is whether those reporting abuse have, in fact, been abused. Leon Jaroff, writing "Lies of the Mind" in *Time* reports that many cases of suspected child abuse, remembered by adults, are not repressed memories as claimed, but the creation of well-meaning but poorly trained therapists.

According to Jaroff, families have been ripped apart by allegations of abuse that parents and family members deny. But the memories are so detailed that law enforcement officials have arrested the alleged perpetrators.

When investigators have attempted to corroborate these stories of abuse, they sometimes have failed. Further research shows that no memories of the abuse existed until the therapist made the suggestion in repeated questioning of the patient. Only after the suggestion is made, do the memories begin to surface, some of them so rich in detail that investigators do not question the validity of them.

Further research, however, suggests that these events did not take place. They are the direct result of suggestions made by the therapist. What this means, simply, is that we don't know much about the working of the human mind.

Thus, there is no way to determine how life experience affects a near-death experience. The power of suggestion might explain the visions of hell that a few people have reported. Or, it might be that the vision of hell is no more real than the vision of demons the woman claimed had come to drag her into hell.

For the vast majority of people who have NDEs, the experience was a positive force in their lives. They have found answers to questions, they are waiting patiently for their chance to repeat the experience and they are no longer frightened.

For those few who are now more frightened, we can only hope that the next time, they will find things more pleasant. It seems unlikely that the events after death would vary so greatly, unless there is something more we don't understand. Of course, that is possible . . . but then, this whole phenomenon is something that we don't understand.

Eight

The Near-Death Experience and the Native American View

For those of us of a European heritage, or from many of the cultures developed in Asia and Africa, the near-death experience is something relatively new and different. Discussion of it didn't begin until the mid-1970s. In the distant past, the Egyptians believed that death was a passage from our world into another. In remote Tibet, the *Tibetan Book of the Dead* provided those who were dying with a map for how to do it properly, with skill and grace.

Although it wasn't written down until about the eighth century A.D., it had been handed down for centuries prior to that as an oral tradition. It provides instruction on what will happen to those who die and provides comfort for those left behind. Interestingly, it outlines the near-death experience as it is defined today. There is, for example, discussion of the out of body experience, in which the newly dead individual learns how to pass through solid objects. There is discussion of a being of pure light, which the dying individual is counseled to approach with feelings of compassion and love. And, there is discussion that there may be others around the one dying, in a state similar to that being experienced.

The *Tibetan Book of the Dead* includes many of the aspects now being reported in the near-death phenomenon, as well as information that goes much further than anything experienced by those who have modern NDEs. But it isn't the only source of that kind of spiritual information. Many of the Native American cultures contain spiritual aspects that mirror the NDE. It is used by them in understanding the world around them.

While those in cultures derived from Europe or modern Asia and Africa experience near-death as a result of trauma of some sort, or a nearly fatal illness, many Native American cultures can create a "near-death" state through meditation and fasting. They view the spiritual world as a resource to be tapped for information. They have established procedures and ceremonial rituals that allow them to cross from this world to the other almost at will. The preparation can take as long as four days, according to some of them, but once the ritualistic cleansing is complete, they then make the journey.

The Mesquaki Indians of central Iowa, for example, fast for four days before "crossing over" to confer with the spirits. Advice and guidance for those in this world is provided by those in the other.

The important thing is that many of the elements of the near-death experience are recounted when interviews are conducted. It is believed that the information is of a "personal" nature and the experience is considered private. They are reluctant to speak at length about what is seen on the other side, or the rituals used to prepare for the experience because they view it as a violation of the conditions under which the information and observations were made.

Other Native Americans also discuss the near-death experience, or rather events that parallel the NDE. Although they might not proceed through a dark tunnel to arrive at the other side, they often report that they travel through a tunnel of light. They are met on the other side by the spirits of their ancestors. In our culture, we speak of meeting family or friends who have preceded us in death. We don't use the word *spirit* but we are discussing the same thing. Their guides are family or friends who had preceded them in death and are now members of the spirit world.

In this spirit world, according to some Native

Americans, there are beings of light. Ancient spirits who have gained great wisdom through long association with Earth and having traveled over it many times in many incarnations. These spirits relate exactly to the "guides" that Betty Eadie described during her near-death experience. They are Ancient Ones filled with knowledge.

The world around them is one of brightness and beauty. The Mesquakis believe the passage to the other side is through the sun. Others believe that the passage is through caves in the Mount Shasta area in California. These passages can be accessed when the proper rituals have been fulfilled.

While on the other side, they ask questions, just as those who experience an NDE have asked dozens of questions. Those questions are often answered. Some of the answers are very specific, providing information on how to live on this side. Other information is more vague, open to interpretation by those who gathered it.

The major difference between the near-death experience and the communication with the spirits as outlined by many of the Native American religions is that those participating in the rituals know they will return to this side. It is not through error that they are on the other side, but through a carefully orchestrated ritual. They have crossed over briefly for a purpose.

It seems that we of the European background

are "forced" into these situations through trauma. The Native Americans are able to access the information voluntarily. In fact, one of those sharing experiences with me used many terms that relate to information retrieval in the computer world. The other side is an area that can be "accessed" to provide "data" for those on this side.

Again, while the near-death experience is happenstance, and the information gathered is accidentally retrieved, Native Americans attempt to learn specific things. They have created the situation rather than letting it happen to them. And they created it in order to find answers.

They do have, however, a tradition of the near-death experience. These match those told by others in that they are induced by trauma and not by ritual. But, they use those experiences as guides for their behavior in this world as well. They have a better understanding of what has happened to them. Because of their beliefs they do not question the experience, searching for a scientific explanation for it. Rather, they interpret it, as do many others who have NDEs, as a "gift" providing them with a different perspective to life here.

Furthermore, many of the Native American religions encompass a belief and an acceptance of reincarnation. Not only can they create a situation where they can experience near-death, they also accept the idea that we have all lived before. Interestingly, one of the members of the Mesquaki tribe mentioned that he believed that each Mesquaki returns to the tribe in each incarnation rather than seeking other life experiences.

While others may believe in a reincarnation that involves a return as a lower form, insects or animals, he believed that humans returned as humans, and Mesquakis returned as Mesquakis. The spirits visited by those who voluntarily cross over are those who have themselves lived on Earth several times.

The point is that the Native Americans believe that their religious core is what provides them with the information they need. While we search for scientific answers, they look to the spiritual world. And, according to them, their answers are often as logical and useful as those found in the scientific world.

We can gain access to some of this spiritual information. People practicing past-life regressions have learned to find that information buried deep in their subconscious minds. Sometimes the trauma of the past has manifested itself in the present, and by knowing that, changes can be made to improve a present life.

But we are unable voluntarily to experience near-death. What we can learn from those native cultures is that there are ways to do it. A guide could be created so that many of us could cross over voluntarily. The problem is that the Native Americans view this information as private much in the same way that Christian religions have private rituals. It is part of their traditional religion and is not to be shared with outsiders. The rituals are complex and are important to the continuing life of their society. Violations of these rituals would compromise their importance and lead to the destruction of their culture, according to their system of beliefs.

However, it does suggest that there might be less than deadly methods of studying the near-death phenomenon. It suggests there are other methods of accessing the data. While we must rely on a traumatic experience to create the circumstances, others, more in tune with the world around them, can find pathways into that other world.

Until we have a better understanding of the world around us, we may find ourselves on the outside looking in. Until we learn that not everything can by classified, analyzed, duplicated, and explained, we're going to be searching for answers. There are some things that have no real answers. There may be some things that we are not meant to know.

Nine

The Near-Death Experience and Christianity

When one examines the near-death phenomenon, one imagines that theologians should embrace the idea. Christianity preaches there is life after death and if there are those who glimpse it, it would seem that this would underscore the validity of those teachings. Although most church leaders reject the idea of "normal" people seeing Jesus or God and conversing with them, the circumstances surrounding the near-death phenomenon would negate some of those objections.

For many, a near-death experience is not followed by a new commitment to traditional religion. These individuals are not inclined to attend church any more frequently. They do not view their experience as religious in nature. But there does seem to be a correlation between the religious beliefs of an individual and the reported aspects of the near-death experience.

Yet almost no traditional Christian churches

view near-death as an "real" experience. They see it as something other, possibly psychological in nature. Few church leaders are excited by reports of near-death experiences, ignoring the implications of them and sticking with the traditional religious dogma. They have little interest in pursuing the phenomenon. They leave study of it to the medical doctors and psychologists.

In fact, most religious writers follow the dictates of the skeptics where addressing the phenomenon at all. They prefer to quote from those suggesting that near-death is nothing more than a brain reacting to the stress of dying.

This seems to be a strange reaction from a group that studies the appearances of the Virgin Mary, Jesus, and subscribes to the idea that miracles . . . God's intervention . . . are real. Instead, they seem to reject the idea of near-death out of hand, either not discussing it intelligently, or relegating it to those who are easily led, telling them that no such thing exists.

An article in *Christianity Today* (October 7, 1988), said, "If Moody's (Dr. Raymond Moody) composite NDE is taken to be a revelation of life after death, it is, in some significant respects, not what Christianity has traditionally taught it to be."

The article continues, saying, "If the apostle Paul, for example, found death in one way attractive—it would allow him to 'be with Christ' (Phil. 1:23)—he largely viewed it as an adversary, the 'last enemy' (1 Cor. 15:26). For Paul, as for the Hebrews before him, death was the unnatural fruit of sin. Judgment followed it, and with judgment, the fearful possibility of eternal separation from God."

The argument seems to be that because Paul argued against death being attractive and that it was the fruit of sin, then the NDE must not be a true representation of what happens after death. The problem with the argument is that Paul did not have a near-death experience. He was arguing a point of view from the rational perspective of those who have never experienced a NDE, nor who realized that such things existed.

There is, however, a suggestion of historical precedent for near-death experiences, Carol Zaleski, a Harvard University lecturer in religion, in her doctoral research, (and later in her book, *Otherworld Journeys: Accounts of Near-Death Experience in Medieval and Modern Times*, Oxford University Press) compared the modern NDE with accounts taken from medieval records. She writes, "However profound and authentic the near-death experience may be, it's not a direct, unmediated experience of the afterlife; it's culturally shaped."

Discussion of the cultural nature of the phenomenon has been made elsewhere, but it is important to remember that some believe that those who experience the NDE report it as best they can in the words they know. It is interesting that the NDEs tend to reflect the vision of heaven that those experiencing them already have. In Micronesia, for example, the NDEs tend to be bright and noisy, often compared to the visions of American cities held by the individuals there.

The argument is that the experience itself is so overwhelming, and the individual is so unable to describe adequately the experience, that cultural elements are injected in an attempt to communicate with others. But the essential elements of the NDE are such that they seem to transcend cultural bias, and any argument about the legitimacy of the phenomenon that relies on a cultural argument is flawed.

Zaleski, in her work, compares a modern American NDE with that of a sixth-century holy man. By examining these two events, a conclusion can be drawn and that conclusion suggests a cultural bias.

While there is some crossover from both the modern and the medieval, "most counts . . . break down when their content is compared. The *Christianity Today* article reports, "So, though both modern and medieval NDEs feature the soul departing the body, each has different imagery for the soul. Medieval accounts often imagine the soul as a homunculus, a small, childlike, and innocent figure. Modern accounts, on the other hand, refer to the soul with quasi-scientific language borrowed from electricity and magnetism."

Zaleski going even farther, said, in a discussion of *Is There Life After Life* by Jonathan Cott, "It's kind of a myth-making process. The book, *Life After Life*, for example, actually stamped on the public imagination a fixed image of what happens at death . . . so much so that a near-death experiencer, who appeared on "The Merv Griffin Show," said that when she had some sort of near-death crisis, she found herself outside of her body but was confused because she hadn't gone through a tunnel and she knew she was 'supposed' to do so."

Of course, that doesn't mean anything specifically about the reality of the near-death experience and Zaleski is quick to point out that the events are "real" to those who report them. She said, ". . . I believe that near-death experiences do occur and are genuine . . ."

Which is saying that the problem is the interpretation of those events, not only by those having them, but by those reporting on them. Moody, among others, believes they show an accurate picture of what happens after death. Others believe there are legitimate scientific explanations for what happens during a near-death experience. The problem, again, is communication by those trying to explain what they saw, felt and experienced. The lack of common ground may be easily explainable as the inability of those having them to tell others about them, and to being limited by the images and descriptions available to them based on their culture, education, and period of existence.

And, while it is possible for us to question those having near-death experiences today, we must rely on the written record of those who have since passed. If we could question them, and if they had access to a modern vocabulary that contained the concepts of electricity and magnetism, then those elements might be present in their discussions. Some psychologists have ascribed the cultural bias to nothing more sinister than the inability of people to describe the events properly, because of the cultural "restrictions" of the language they use.

In many Christian publications, and in some Christian thought, the NDE is a manifestation of Satan. Cott, in his article in *Vogue*, mentioned that "Some conservative Christian theologians have called books like *Life After Life* 'Satan Tricks.' . . . As one critic put it, 'There is no need for Easter if we are immortal.' "

Zaleski, responding to those comments, mentioned that many religious experiences revolve around the concept of "being judged, of being held accountable . . . all of which is missing in the life-after-life emphasis on the beneficent beings you'll encounter . . ."

But that doesn't respond to the criticism that it is somehow a Satanic activity, almost as if to admit Satanic influence would underscore the reality of the NDE. But nothing in those experiences suggests anything Satanic. With few exceptions, these experiences all have positive effects on the lives of those who have them. They might not become better Christians, but they do become better people and isn't that really the point?

In Clapp's *Christianity Today* article, it is noted that "The apparent dismissal of orthodox Christianity and the plunge into New Age currents by some researchers . . . have caused some Christians to ascribe NDEs to the Devil and leave it at that. Yet there are problems with that response."

And one of the problems is that it explains nothing, but allows Christians to reject the near-death experience without having to think about it. Too many times, that which they don't understand, or don't want to understand, is the work of Satan—including everything from space flight to television and most other modern conveniences. While the presence of Satan "explains" some the problems of the world, it answers no questions.

Christian theology, however, has other explanations for the near-death experience. *Christianity Today* asks the question, "The NDE: Any theological usefulness?" The answer, according to them is, "Not much."

Again, falling back on the work of Zaleski, the near-death experience in the Middle Ages is examined. Zaleski believes that the NDE fell out of favor in medieval times because of the Reformation. According to her, a wide variety of practices and ideas were rejected in favor of a "pure biblical faith."

Christian thought today seems to underscore that instinct by Reformers. According to *Christianity Today*, "There is no solid theological reason Christians should desire a surer witness to the reality of life beyond death than the resurrection of Jesus Christ."

Continuing in that vein, Clapp writes, "He [Paul] bases his trust that there is life after death squarely on the resurrection of Christ: 'If Christ has not been raised, your faith is futile and you are still in your sins. Then those also who have fallen asleep in Christ have perished.' (1 Cor. 15:17-18)."

But, Clapp admits to some theological usefulness, pointing out that "They prove nothing in and of themselves, but here and there they open the spiritual realm to those who previously ignored it." He continues, ". . . as the surge of enthusiasm about New Age channeling and other practices shows, there are dangers when the undiscriminating are awakened to the spiritual world. But at the very least, its acknowledgement is an entree for sober theological discussion of a reality transcending what we can see with our eyes and touch with our fingers."

What we're seeing is a rejection of the phenomenon of near-death by the theological world. Although they condemn the reliance on science, or the expression of beliefs in a material sense, they use those concepts when dealing with near death. Rather than view it as a glimpse of the afterlife, or as a reaffirmation of their beliefs, they tend to view it as a threat to them.

Although they concede that some of those who experience NDE "return to the fold" or find faith, or even convert atheists to Christianity, they don't accept the events as "real." Instead, they return to the psychological dogma to persuade those unfamiliar with the literature on the topic that near death means nothing in a spiritual sense.

In some camps they argue the "logic" of the situation. If near-death experiences are true, and if the situation after death is so magnificent, then why don't those who have had it commit suicide to return to it? In other words, those people don't have the courage of their convictions.

But, as Tom Dolembo pointed out, he doesn't know what is on the other side. He has seen part of it, but still wants to experience some of the material aspects of this world. A beautiful day is something to be enjoyed because there are a finite number of them. He won't rush to cross to the other side, but neither does he fear it.

Rather than use the NDE as a way of reinforcing the faith of those who are flagging, it seems that Christianity is built on the idea that you must accept by faith. A true Christian is one who believes in Christ and life after death because of his or her faith. But most of us don't have that kind of faith, and if a NDE helps underscore that faith, then what, one might ask, is wrong with it?

Dolembo said that he had no respect for organized religions, and, with history on his side, that is understandable. Many horrible things have been done in the name of Christ. That is not to say that there is something wrong with Christianity, but rather with some of those who profess to be Christians. Even if Christ had never walked the Earth, the lessons he taught would be valuable in making this a better world. Unfortunately those lessons have sometimes been perverted by those who think they act in the name of Christ.

Organized religions turn a skeptical eye to the near-death phenomenon, possibly fearing it will erode the faithful. But it seems that many who have experienced NDE have seen Christ and had their faith reinforced. Although few would express it in these terms, they have become better Christians because of the experience and isn't that the most important aspect of it?

Instead of studying this, traditional Christian leaders want to reject it, lumping the near-death phenomena with sensational stories in supermarket tabloids, the implication being that there is something less than honest or credible about the reports of NDE. But that tactic achieves little more than guilt by association and has no real relevance to the NDE.

Those who have near-death experiences do not forget their Christianity, if they began as Christians; nor are Moslems converted to Christianity by a NDE. Their descriptions differ, not because the experience is different, but because their culture is different and they describe the events using different words.

The point is that theological thought suggests that NDEs are a result of the physiological processes of death and have nothing to do with Christianity or the afterlife. They argue against near-death experience, suggesting that Moody, for example, is engaged in myth-making, or citing examples from TV talk shows rather than the evidence gathered by credible researchers.

In the end, however, it will be up to each individual to decide if NDEs reinforce or detract from their faith. It would seem that all Christians would embrace the light because it provides a measure of comfort and while it might be considered "Unchristian" to want proof, it certainly does not make those people any less Christian.

Ten

The Near-Death Experience and Science

The scientific community, naturally, can explain the near-death phenomenon in very basic scientific terms. Several psychologists have studied those reporting near-death, and believe that it is possible to explain all that is seen and reported, inside the framework of contemporary science. In fact, they insist, the reports are similar to a number of other well-defined psychological phenomena.

Dr. Barry Beyerstein, a psychology professor at Simon Fraser University in Burnaby, B.C., was quoted in *McLean's* (April 20, 1992) as saying, "The experiences are sufficiently like other states so it's better to assume that they are things the brain is capable of generating under certain circumstances." He added, "I think it's probably a bad idea to mix science and religion."

Paul Kurtz, chairman of the Committee for Scientific Investigation of Claims of the Paranormal wrote in *Psychology Today* (September 1988), "Medical science can now resuscitate patients who have suffered cardiac arrest, who have stopped breathing and who have little discernible brain activity—people, that is to say, who years ago would have died. Personal tales of NDEs make fascinating reading, and there is no reason to doubt the honesty or accuracy of these accounts. But many take a further leap and interpret these experiences as a glimpse into 'the other side.' "

Kurtz had put his finger directly on the problem for those studying the near-death phenomenon. While the witnesses are relating, honestly, what they have experienced themselves, it is the interpretation of those experiences that science questions. The crux of the problem is to design a scientific study that could, somehow, take the interpretation out of the experiences and provide science with something that could be duplicated in the laboratory and measured by a variety of instruments. Without that, we are left with the anecdotal musings that science so rightly abhors.

In fact, Kurtz goes further still, explaining that there are some "fundamental problems with the notion that survivors have actually experienced death . . . There is a basic confusion about the definition of death, which in recent years has been revised to mean complete brain death . . . No reliable evidence exists to show that people who report such experiences [NDEs] have died and returned . . ."

With these problems outlined, is there anything that can be said that doesn't rely on a "leap of faith?" Can we draw any conclusions at all?

We can examine the near-death experience and compare it to other human experiences. For example Ronald Siegel, a research associate professor at UCLA, writes in his book *Fire in the Brain: Clinical Tales of Hallucination,* that hallucinations can be triggered by fear, loneliness or isolation. It could be, that when the brain is close to death, it reacts to the threat with fantasies.

In other words, those who have experienced the sudden calming effects of the bright light, the pleasant memories induced by a voice from the past, and the feeling of well-being—have experienced nothing more than a defense mechanism of the brain. These effects are similar to the effects of mind-altering drugs such as LSD.

Rev. Albert Moraczewski, according to Nora Underwood, (*McLean's* April 20, 1988) concluded that the "experiences are probably the result of metabolic changes, such as temporary oxygen deprivation or a sudden release of hormones in the body. Moraczewski also notes the similarity between near-death experiences and the effects of some hallucinogenic drugs."

Moraczewski also said, ". . . the church would

object to it [near-death experiences] being seen as an encounter with Christ or God in a direct sense."

Various segments of the religious community have investigated claims of near-death experience among their members. It would seem that they might be more inclined to accept the testimony of their religious brothers and sisters, over the pronouncements of the scientific community, but such doesn't seem to be the case. A review of the Betty Malz case is illustrative of that view.

Christianity Today investigated Betty Malz's near-death experience as reported in her book, *My Glimpse of Eternity*. Ken Sidey wrote that "a recent article in *Christian Week* . . . calls into question the truthfulness of the story on which Malz [a sixty-four-year-old Assemblies of God member who conducts women's retreats] has built her ministry. Medical personnel involved in the case, quoted in the article, say Betty Malz did not die."

Here was a religious magazine looking into the phenomenon of near-death, but they avoided, for the most part, the religious aspects of the case. Instead they focused on the credibility of Malz and the possible corroboration of her story.

Malz had claimed that she had been in a coma for forty-four days and that during the night, a nurse, checking her vital signs found that she had died. According to Malz, at 5:00 A.M., she was pronounced dead by a doctor and a sheet was pulled over her face, the room left in darkness.

Two days after she "died" she was sent home, and she reported no after-effects of the trauma. She believed that a prayer from her father had been answered.

Lorna Dueck, researching an article for *Christian Week*, attempted to verify Malz's story. She went to Terre Haute, Indiana, where Malz claimed the near-death experience took place. Speaking to Dr. Henry Bopp, who twice performed surgery on Malz, she learned, "This is almost a complete fabrication . . . She did not die. She may have dreamt she did, but she did not die in the hospital."

In fact, James Bopp (brother of Henry Bopp), who was the anesthetist during Malz's surgery, said, "I challenge [the publishers] to produce the medical records . . ."

The publisher, Chosen Books, said that it would stand by the book and the author. They claim that the hospital wants to cover up for their handling of the case.

Dueck, in her search, checked with hospital sources, and learned that Malz had, indeed, been in the hospital during July 1959 when she "died" but that there were two stays totalling only twenty-nine days and not forty-four as she said. The day she "died" is the day that she was discharged.

Dueck even found Malz's attending physician, Dr. H. Clark Boyd, who said that he had expected a reporter to find and question him long ago. He confirmed that his patient had been sick, but had not been in a coma and had not "died" at any time during her treatment.

Malz was challenged to produce her medical records by *Christianity Today* but she refused, saying that she wanted to put the whole mess behind her.

Chosen Books co-founder, Leonard LeSourd told investigators for *Christianity Today* that he had edited Malz's book and had even gone to Terre Haute in 1976 to verify the information in the book. LeSourd confirms that the medical people he interviewed denied that Malz had died, but said, ". . . the doctors would say that. I expected them to be defensive for fear of medical malpractice [lawsuits]."

Interestingly, Sidey, in his article, draws no real conclusion, other than to quote from Jane Campbell, a Chosen Books editor. "If she was promoting a story that were not true . . . that would be deplorable. I don't believe she's doing that. If I did, I'd pull the book in a minute."

But the argument here, is not over the interpretation of Malz's experiences, but over the veracity of her claim. Investigators for *Christian*

Week and *Christianity Today* could do nothing other than speak to those involved. They could not run tests, there was nothing for them to measure to determine if Malz was telling the truth as she knew it, and there was no way to verify her story except to check with the hospital records which seemed to contradict Malz.

What strikes a real cord is Malz's refusal to produce her medical records. Although such documents are considered private and not available to the general public, Malz certainly could release them. They would go a long way to verify her story. Instead, she just wants to put the "controversy" behind her. That suggests the records either don't exist, or, that they are in conflict with Malz and her story. If they don't confirm her story, then her book is badly flawed.

That is the trend for investigation of these claims. Because there is nothing for science to measure, there are no observations that can be conducted inside a controlled, laboratory environment. The only avenue for most investigation is the background of those reporting the events.

Or, science can compare the near-death experience with other, documented events. Kurtz reinforced this, writing, "There are any number of explanations for the variety of encounters that make up NDEs. NDEs are not unlike other out-of-body experiences (OBEs) that are commonly encountered and do not occur in near-death situations."

Other researchers, many of them independent, claim that all this does not fully account for what happens to the witnesses who report near-death events. Dr. Bruce Greyson, interviewed for *McLean's* said, "That doesn't mean there isn't a psychological explanation . . . just that we haven't found one."

There have been many reports of near-death, by a cross section of the population. Estimates suggest that nearly eight million people have had some sort of a near-death experience. The problem is that only so much can be learned from anecdotal evidence. After scientists, psychologists and researchers have gathered the experiences of a dozen, two dozen, a hundred or a thousand people, nothing new is learned. There are always variations which could be easily explained in terms of cultural diversity, personal observations, and educational levels of those making the reports.

A few suggestions have been made, but it boils down to a lack of independent, verifiable events. Scientists are hard-pressed to design experiments that can be conducted with the safety of the subject kept in mind, and in an environment where the subjects can be controlled. After all, for it to work, they would have to literally kill the subject and then hope that attempts at resuscitation would be successful.

One scientist has suggested that a large group of people who are at risk for heart attacks be thoroughly studied. If any of the people in the group was later resuscitated, then their experiences could be documented at the time of resuscitation. Instrumentation available at hospitals could answer many questions about their "deaths" such as whether they were clinically dead, physically dead, or brain dead. It might provide insight into the process of dying rather than the actual state of death but even that information would be useful.

But again, the question becomes: Are the subjects experiencing an event that is taking place? Is it a hallucination induced by the brain, or by chemicals released to the brain, or by contamination from the number of books and articles dealing with near-death? Or is the phenomenon something that science currently fails to understand?

There are "cultural universals" scattered throughout the near-death experience. A cultural universal is a legend, story, explanation that transcends a single culture. The story of a great flood seems to be a cultural universal. Every culture, regardless of location, time of existence, or extent of communication with other cultures has had an account of a great flood.

In the near-death experience there are certain things that are reported over and over. Most people report changes in their personal system of values. Things that were important to them, often the material aspect of life, have changed radically. Now relationships with others are more important than gathering material wealth. They have a new concept about love and they seem to be more relaxed about life in general. Nearly all of them report that they no longer fear death, though some say they fear dying. Dying, according to them can be ugly and brutal, but once the process is over, death itself is wonderful.

There are, however, a few who do not experience the pleasant feelings and the love radiating from the light. Nancy Evans Bush has been collecting near-death experiences for a dozen years and reports that a few people are frightened by their near-death experiences. There are three types of these experiences. First are those of people who say it was pleasant, but they were upset by what they believed was their loss of control. Second, is a group that sees "a great cosmic nothingness." No friends or family, no comforting light, and a sense of being caught in a void. Finally, there are those who believe they have glimpsed hell, with scenes of people in torment and being tortured.

A few researchers, according to an article in *Psychology Today* (July/August 1992) written by James Mauro, have wondered if the NDE is a cultural universal. Do other people in other parts of the world report the same sorts of experiences?

Dr. Nsama Mumbwe, of the University of Zambia, studied fifteen people from that African nation who reported near death. He learned that many of the Africans believed that the events were somehow evil or that they were bewitched. Japanese report long, dark rivers, and, as mentioned earlier, East Indians believe heaven to be a giant bureaucracy and are sent back because of clerical errors (not unlike the problems from the movie *Heaven Can Wait*), and those from Micronesia claim that heaven is like a large American city filled with light and noise.

Dr. Melvin Morse, a pediatrician from Seattle, along with other researchers, doesn't see these interpretations as significantly different. Many of those who have had near-death experiences report they can't find the proper words to describe what they had seen or felt. They can only draw on the vocabulary and images of their own worldly culture to try to recount this most unworldly experience so that others will understand. Mauro wrote, ". . . the similarities across a wide variety of cultures, ages, and religions support the idea that being near death not only triggers a specific type of experience, but that the experience is 'transcendental.' "

But, again, these are the interpretations of those undergoing the experience and may not reflect reality. That is the real problem.

There are those skeptics who have been converted. Raymond Moody, who has authored a number of books on near-death and who is credited with inventing the term, reports that skeptics tried to prove him wrong and ended up believing in the reality of NDEs themselves.

More than one of them was convinced of the reality of near death because the patient could describe, in amazing detail, the attempts to resuscitate him or her. Paul Perry, writing about "Brushes with Death" in *Psychology Today* reported that Dr. Michael Sobom conducted a survey of those who claimed near-death and those who had been resuscitated but who made no reports of a near-death experience.

What he learned was that of those who had near-death experiences, the majority of them could accurately describe the events that transpired around them. Of those who did not describe an "out of body" experience, but who were questioned about the resuscitation and the efforts of the doctors and nurses in the emergency room, the majority made major errors in their descriptions.

Skeptics, however, point out that even people who have lost consciousness have an awareness of the events around them. Surgeons tell of many patients, assumed to be unconscious during surgery, who can describe what was said by the doctors and nurses, and even some of the technical procedures that were performed.

Sobom said, "I don't think this stuff should be sensationalized . . . It should be looked at as part of the normal living and dying process."

Others suggest that even if the near-death experience is not a glimpse into the "after life" there might be something in them that "might advance therapeutic methods for all kinds of problems—from the dilemmas of suicidal patients to the enduring [emotional] pain of those who have been abused as children," according to Mauro.

As the arguments continue, there are those who believe that the near-death phenomenon might have a chemical cause. Morse said that there had long been a "medical school bias" against near-death experiences. Doctors believed that the reports were the result of hallucinations. A Canadian neurosurgeon, Wilder Penfield, identified the part of the brain responsible for the near-death experience. By stimulating areas of the temporal lobe, the patients recalled vivid memories, reporting that they could "see" the memories.

Some researchers now believe that endorphins cause the euphoria and glimpses of heaven reported, that compression of the optic nerve is responsible for the "tunnel" vision, and that the neurotransmitter serotonin, released under the stress of dying, is the cause of the near-death phenomenon.

Other researchers such as Dr. Ian Stevenson

and Dr. Justine Owens have wondered if those reporting near-death experiences were actually near death. They speculated that patients, believing they were near death, might have had the experience. They termed it "fear death."

One study of the medical records of forty patients who had reported near-death, found that, according to the records, more than half were not close to dying. It was the belief that triggered the event and not the actual trauma of dying.

Stevenson and Owens, to their credit, didn't stop there. They interviewed fifty-eight people, of whom just over fifty percent had not been near death. But what surprised them was that those who had actually been near death reported the core elements, that is the bright light and feelings of calm. Those who had only believed they were close to death failed to report many of the core elements of the near death experience.

Some of these researchers believe that the NDE is actually a "disassociation" not unlike that experienced by abused children. Unable to cope with the situation, they separate themselves from the trauma, looking down on the situation from somewhere else. In that way they are no longer a part of what is happening to them. There has been a great deal of research into disassociation which, according to some psychologists, can lead to the development of multiple personalities.

Comparing the near-death experience with the childhood memories of abuse, researchers have discovered a number of common traits. But the question becomes, are the out-of-body experiences real, or are they merely a defense thrown up by the mind to protect itself.

But none of this discussion provides answers to the real questions. Studies of those who believe they have been close to death or believe they have died, are merely studies of the people who have reported what they saw. Science is unable to do anything else because of the nature of the phenomenon. In fact, some scientists get caught in arguments over semantics in their attempt to learn what is happening during a near-death experience. One scientist said that someone who swerved to avoid a traffic accident has had a "near death" experience for it is quite possible for him to have been killed in the crash. But that is a poor analogy for the experiences of so many people who have undergone some very traumatic episodes.

Scientists realize the limitations of their research. They're never going to obtain hard physical evidence of life after death. The very nature of the question makes it impossible to answer. They can explain, in scientific terms, what they believe is happening, but science often tries to explain the functioning of the world in scientific terms when such terms and explanations may be irrelevant. A thousand years ago mystics explained the functioning of the world with superstitions that made sense to them. Learned men taught what they had observed themselves and created "natural" laws that allowed them to predict the functioning of the world around them.

We have strayed from mysticism, and rightly so. But science cannot explain many of the things of our world. Scientists may expose frauds—people who claim to have ESP, telekinetic ability, or who claim to have had contact with the "spirit" world—but scientists sometimes fail to explain these phenomena precisely. They label them a hoax, as if the label somehow explains everything.

With the near-death experience, science can provide some interesting alternative ideas. Chemical reactions in the brain, traumatic stimulation to protect the brain, and hallucination can explain near-death to those with a scientific frame of mind.

Of course, the transcendental nature of the experience is just as plausible. In either case, those interested are required to accept, on faith, the pronouncements of those they want to believe. It comes down to, in some cases, how you want to invest your faith . . . in science, which has led us from the dark ages and into the light, or in those people who tell us that beyond the darkness of death there is a bright light.

In the end, science argues about what is the truth, with dedicated people lining up on both sides. They all agree that those telling of their near-death experiences are, for the most part, honest people relating truthfully what they have witnessed. The question that hasn't been answered is what they witnessed. Was it a chemical reaction in the brain or was it a real glimpse of what is beyond the light on the other side.

Part III:
Reincarnation

Eleven

The Continued Search for Bridey Murphy

Closely related to the near-death experience is the concept of reincarnation. Both concepts incorporate something, maybe the soul, surviving death. Both suggest that a consciousness is carried to the other side, and as Tom Dolembo, among others, suggested, there is a personal identity that is carried from this side to the other.

Most references to reincarnation were edited out of the King James version of the Bible because it did not fit into the Christian doctrine of that time. Reincarnation belonged to ancient civilizations such as the Egyptians, or to ancient religions such as Hinduism.

The point, however, is that reincarnation was not accepted in Christian circles. Today, when most people are asked about their concept of reincarnation, they suggest that it is the idea that we come back as an animal or plant. Although some of the world's religions do embrace that idea, it is only the truly evil who come back as an animal or lower life form. Most, who believe in reincarnation, believe that each of us returns many times to live many lives. This is, according to the doctrine, a growing experience for all of us. That is the purpose. To allow us to grow.

The idea of reincarnation splashed across headlines in this country in the mid-1950s when Morey Bernstein published *The Search for Bridey Murphy*. Murphy, according to Bernstein, was a woman who had lived in the early- to mid-nineteenth century in Ireland and who died in 1864. Bernstein had met Murphy after she died, while performing a hypnotic regression experiment on a woman he labeled as Ruth Simmons (her real name has been printed since then, but I see no point in using it here so I will use the name created by Bernstein) from Colorado.

Bernstein had met Simmons earlier at a party and hypnotized her. He realized that she was a good subject, since she could slip into a hypnotic state quickly and easily. Later, as he learned about reincarnation, first from an acquaintance, and then from the teachings of Edgar Cayce and the Association for Research and Enlightenment, he decided to try hypnotically to find "memories before birth." His first task was to find a proper subject for his experiment, one who could be placed in a deep trance so that she would not consciously remember what had happened under the influence of hypnosis. Bernstein's first choice had left for the Navy, so he finally settled on Simmons.

Because he wasn't well acquainted with Ruth, or her husband Rex, it took several weeks to set up the appointment. As Bernstein wrote in his book, "I was forced to compete with bridge games, cocktail parties and club dances." Finally, his patience was rewarded, and he met with Simmons for the purpose of learning if he could take her back, into another life.

According to Bernstein, he first made her comfortable, then with a tape recorder running, he began the session.

He began by regressing her to an earlier age, and asked her what she was seeing. She described a scene from her early childhood while she was in school. He then tried to take her back, deeper and deeper into her past, until she was six, or four, and finally one. Then Bernstein told her that she could remember times before she was one. Bernstein said, "Oddly enough, you can go even farther back. I want you to keep on going back and back in your mind. And, surprising as it may seem, strange as it may seem, you will find that there are other scenes in your memory. There are other scenes from faraway lands and distant places in your memory."

When Bernstein asked her what she was seeing, Simmons began to speak of a life that preceded the one she was now living. She told

Bernstein that her name was Bridey (Bridget Kathleen Murphy, born December 20, 1798) and that she lived in Cork, Ireland. At first, Bernstein misunderstood her, thinking that she said her name was Friday. She told Bernstein, and those assembled in the room, that she had scratched the paint off her metal bed. She had been punished for that.

Bernstein tried to probe deeper and Simmons, as Bridey Murphy was able to answer questions about her life in Ireland, giving the names of her father, mother and brothers. When asked, she told Bernstein that the year was 1802. She also said that she was only four years old.

Moving forward in time, Bernstein learned more about the life of Bridey Murphy. She described her house, and spoke of playing with her brother. She said that she had another brother, but that he'd died while still an infant.

As Bridey Murphy, Simmons described what they ate, and how they lived. She revealed that her father was a barrister. Bernstein found the use of that word interesting because, to Americans, all barristers are lawyers. Under the English system, different types of attorneys are ranked. Bernstein was surprised that a fairly young American woman would use a term more properly used in Great Britain.

Murphy provided Bernstein with a wealth of detail about her life. She said that she had been named for her grandmother and that was why she was called Bridey instead of Bridget.

She talked about her schooling at Mrs. Strayne's Day School. The curriculum was limited to "house things . . and proper things."

She also spoke of her husband, Brian Mac-Carthy, who, according to Murphy, was still going to school. Brian's father was a barrister, too.

Murphy didn't have children and after marrying Brian, she moved from Cork to Belfast. She mentioned friends she had in Belfast, the name of the priest at her church as well as the name of the church.

Simmons, speaking as Murphy, told of her death at age sixty-six. She had fallen down the stairs and broken several bones. After she died, she didn't "go" away. Instead, she stayed in her house watching her husband, apparently waiting for him. He died many years later.

Interestingly, Murphy described "visiting" her home in Cork after she died. She visited her brother, Duncan, who was still alive. It amazed her that he had survived her. He was "so old" according to her.

Murphy also described seeing her little brother, the one who had died in infancy after her own passing. Her little brother didn't know who she was, and she had to tell him. She also saw Father John.

Bernstein, writing in his book, said that it had never occurred to him that Murphy would be able to describe her . . . "existence" after death. This was an area that he just hadn't thought about.

She told Bernstein where she was during the period between lives. She said that she never had to eat or sleep and that one never got tired. That world, the "spirit" world, according to what Bernstein learned, was a transitory place. "Just a period, just something that happened." She left that world, according to what she said, to be born in Wisconsin. That was the life she was living as Ruth Simmons.

She also recalled a life as a baby in New Amsterdam in the New World, but since she died as an infant, there wasn't much for her to remember. She was able, however, to tell Bernstein, when he asked, that New Amsterdam's name had been changed to New York. Even though she was experiencing, or remembering a life that predated the existence of New York, she was able to bring her knowledge as Ruth Simmons into the sessions. She still had access to the information that Simmons had, even when experiencing an event that was far older than Simmons.

Bernstein used hypnosis on several other occasions to learn more about the life of Bridey Murphy. She was married in 1818, and her husband published some law articles in 1843. She died in 1864 without having children of her own.

Because Murphy lived into the second half of the nineteenth century, there was a chance that there could be records from her life. It was possible, Bernstein believed, to corroborate some of what he had been told. There was some discussion of this in *The Search for Bridey Murphy*. Bernstein told of their luck, or their lack of it.

Once the book was published in January 1956, the critics lined up to attack it. In May and June, a Hearst newspaper, the Chicago *American* printed an exposé, proving that the Bridey Murphy story was a hoax. Other magazines, assuming that the *American* reporters had done their job properly, announced that the search was over . . . "ended by a series of Chicago *American* articles."

Other newspapers and magazines, jumping on the bandwagon, published their own exposés of the Murphy hoax. In one, it was claimed that Simmons had admitted that she had invented the story. Another reported that, "Only after he'd written a best-seller did Bernstein shamefacedly admit that *The Search for Bridey Murphy* belonged on the fiction, not the non-fiction shelves."

The *Denver Post* printed a rebuttal, based on the research done by a feature writer, Bob Byers, who believed that he had shown that most of the exposé material in the Chicago article was "in error." Yet *Life* magazine, in a feature about Murphy, ignored that, reprinting without checking, the story that Murphy was lying about her experiences.

William J. Barker, writing in a paperback edition of *The Search for Bridey Murphy*, reported, "Today, in large part because of the damaging effect of the *Life* piece which circulated the Chicago stuff to millions, many people when the Bridey case comes up in conversation will say, 'Oh, yeah . . . That was proved to be a hoax or something, wasn't it?' " (In fact, when I mentioned it to my mother, she said much the same thing, though I had grown up in Denver.) Barker responds, "In all honesty, no such proof ever has been produced."

In fact, Barker laments that "many articles purporting to give 'the inside facts' on the case popped up in a variety of magazines, books, and tabloids. Invariably the debunking, scoffing line was taken but, the incredible aspect of so many of these 'exposés' was the apparent willingness to substitute so-called experts' opinions for substantiated facts."

Barker takes the "proofs" of Murphy's deceit and exposes them, one by one. For example, the Chicago newspaper, owned by the Hearst corporation, and later the *San Francisco Examiner,* another Hearst newspaper, used the Reverend Wally White as one of its sources because Ruth

Simmons as a young girl had apparently attended his church in Chicago. Barker writes that it makes no difference because White wasn't there when Simmons was. In fact, White had told others that his mission was to "debunk reincarnation." In other words, the claim that White knew Simmons was wrong, but that made no difference to him. White wanted to destroy the story for reasons other than scientific or theological.

Those searching for answers to the Bridey Murphy questions began to reach for their explanations. They suggested that Simmons was well versed in Irish history because she had lived for a time with an aunt who was as Irish as they came, and who had told young Simmons long, involved tales of her life in Ireland. But Simmons's aunt had been born in New York and had no interest in Ireland.

The Chicago newspaper exposé didn't stop there. They "discovered" that a neighbor of Simmons, when she was growing up, was Mrs. Anthony Bridie Murphy Corkell, from County Mayo, Ireland. The supposed similarity in the name, and the fact that Corkell was from Ireland, "proved" to the newspaper that Simmons had received the name Bridey Murphy and the information about Ireland from her neighbor.

Although they thought this coincidence was significant, continued research failed to reveal any other modern connections to the names that Simmons supplied. Corkell lived in the extreme midwestern part of Ireland and Simmons, as Bridey Murphy, lived in southern Ireland and then in northeastern Ireland. In other words, Corkell knew nothing of the territory that Murphy had claimed as home. There is no way that Corkell, if she had ever talked to Simmons, could have supplied the wealth of detail that Simmons gave under hypnosis.

But the real problem is that those who tried to contact Corkell were unable to do so. She refused to take phone calls from reporters, other than those with the Chicago *American*. Finally reporters learned that Corkell's son, John, was the Sunday editor of the Chicago *American*.

And, more importantly, no documentation was ever found suggesting that Corkell's full legal name included any reference to Bridey Murphy. Forced to use church records and friends' memories, no one ever came forward suggesting that Corkell had ever been known as Mrs. Anthony Bridie Murphy Corkell.

Overlooked by the Chicago paper's exposé were the facts that Simmons recalled under hypnosis. These facts could be verified through independent research and documentation—which suggested there was a core of truth to the tale.

Barker, among others, examined the story told by Simmons as Murphy, searching for corroboration. Barker had been sent to Ireland by the *Denver Post* and published his findings in an article called, "The Truth about Bridey Murphy." It appeared on March 11, 1956 in a twelve-page supplement to the newspaper and was later widely reprinted though it was never acknowledged by the national magazines that had used the exposé as the center of their anti-Bridey Murphy stories.

When he began his search, Barker knew some of the problems with hypnosis. He was also cautioned by Bernstein, who told him that he believed that Bridey Murphy stretched the truth. She embellished the lives of her family trying to make them sound more important than they were.

But Barker wasn't warned and may not have realized one critical point. Bernstein, when he began the experiment, had already unwittingly contaminated it. By telling Simmons that she could see farther into the past, back before she was born, he was telling her what he wanted to hear. He was "priming the pump." Today, those using hypnotic regression must be careful about "leading" the subject into a realm they want to discuss. As Barker points out, a person under hypnosis is not under oath. People in a state of hypnosis can and do lie. They are able to draw on all their life experience when attempting to answer questions. This is not limited to what they have lived themselves, but to any books they have read, movies they have seen, or stories they have been told.

Time magazine published a long article on "forced memories." In the last few years hundreds of people have come forward with tales of abuse at the hands of family and friends that have been "long repressed." It is becoming clearer that a therapist, psychologist, or hypnotist can easily lead a subject into a realm that doesn't exist. It is necessary for those to proceed carefully, allowing the subject to remember the details, rather than provide them with leading questions and traumatic therapy sessions. That Simmons found herself in another life was suggested by the hypnotist, and for some, that inadvertent contamination may have biased the case from the start.

Barker, however, made a trip to Ireland searching for corroboration, and his trip and his findings more than negate the possible damage done early on. Of course he didn't have immediate luck. He failed to find the by-line of Brian MacCarthy, Bridey Murphy's husband who, it was claimed, had published writings in the *News-Letters* in Belfast. He found no reference at all to Brian MacCarthy, but then there were few by-lines, no index or cross references, and it would have taken days to make a comprehensive search—with no guarantee that even if MacCarthy had published work in the *News-Letters* there would have been a by-line for Barker to find. That he searched at all is significant. None of those writing the exposés had taken the trouble to question this aspect of the Murphy story.

But others, whom Murphy claimed to have known during her life in Belfast were discovered to have existed. She had mentioned two grocery stores, one called Farr's and the other known as John Carrigan's. Searching the city directory for 1865-66, references to both stores were discovered. Barker wrote that the references were located by Belfast Chief Librarian John Bebbington.

In fact, according to Barker, Bebbington, "made it clear to me that the old directories were far from complete . . . However, both Carrigan and Farr are on record as being the *only* (emphasis in original) individuals of those names engaged in the 'foodstuffs' business . . . How or by what means Ruth Simmons could have obtained this obscure information, when it took Belfast librarians weeks to discover it, defies easy explanation . . ."

Some of objections to the Murphy story were ridiculous. A clergyman wrote an article critical of the whole story, including the ludicrous statement, "She relates how her mother told her about 1810, about kissing the Blarney Stone. The stone existed in Blarney Castle then but the legend about kissing it was created in . . . a poem written about 1840."

Such an argument sounds solid on the surface. Barker, however, examined that as well. He pointed out that no date was given by Murphy for when she first heard the story. The 1810 date was an invention by the clergyman. And, according to Dermont Foley, chief librarian in Cork, "T. Crofton Crocker, in his *Researches in South Ireland,* published in 1824, establishes the custom as having been practiced as least as early as 1820."

Other criticisms of the Murphy story were equally stretched to the limits. When Bernstein, during his first attempt to find a time before Simmons was born, asked what she was doing, Bridey Murphy said that she was scraping the paint off the iron bed when she was four, meaning it happened in 1802. The Chicago *American* reported that iron beds were not available in Ireland until after 1850.

Barker asked many authorities—antique dealers in Ireland—who agreed that metal beds weren't available in 1802. But the *Encyclopedia Britannica* (1950), said, "Iron beds appear in the 18th Century; the advertisements recommend them as free from the insects which sometimes infested wooden bedsteads."

Murphy, in one of the sessions, was asked what her husband was doing after 1847 and she responded that he taught law at Queen's College. The Chicago *American* claimed that this couldn't be true because the Queen's College did not exist until 1849 and Queen's University did not come into existence until 1908.

Again research showed that this was not exactly right. According to *The Belfast Queen's College Calendar* (Catalogue, 1862), Queen Victoria, quoted in the text, said, "We . . . at our Court at St. James's, the nineteenth day of December, one thousand eight hundred and forty-five [December 19, 1845] . . . do ordain . . . there shall and may be erected . . . one college for students in Arts, Law, Physic . . . which shall be called Queen's College, Belfast . . ." The first students arrived October 30, 1849.

On August 15, 1850, Queen Victoria issued another decree, elevating the colleges into a system of universities. In other words, Murphy's husband, Brian, could have taught at the University just as she said because it was the Chicago *American* which assumed that Murphy meant 1848 . . . and Brian could have worked at the college before the students arrived in 1849. Such hair-splitting criticism of the Murphy story does nothing to answer questions about the validity of Ruth Simmons's claims as Murphy.

Where there was no information to prove the point either way, those believing Simmons to be lying decided that the information proved that Simmons was lying. Barker wrote, "For example, the magazine's anonymous reporter wrote, 'She says she lived in a nice house . . . it's a wood house . . . white . . . has two floors . . . and was called 'The Meadows.' " The magazine claimed that there are almost no wooden houses in Ireland because timber is too scarce. Cork is built of stone and brick. The public records, according to the magazine fail to show any house called "The Meadows."

Barker points out that in Ireland today, there are almost no wooden houses. Of course, to say there are almost no wooden houses, isn't the same as there being none.

But the important point is the reference to "The Meadows." No one was able to find out what that meant. It was some sort of an address, but there was nothing in the records that provided a clue about the reference.

Barker had a "beautifully detailed map of Cork, executed by William Beaufort in 1801. The western half of it shows what must have been a very handsome suburban portion of the city formally called Mardike Meadows . . . In The Meadows on the map are a total of seven or eight buildings widely scattered . . . Was one of these Murphy's home? She had said, 'Don't have any neighbors . . . live outside the village.' "

So, even though the evidence is inconclusive about The Meadows and the wooden houses, there is a hint of truth. A truth that would not have been readily available to a woman living in Colorado in the mid-1950s.

The whole point here is that Ruth Simmons, speaking as Bridey Murphy from Cork was able to describe a life in Ireland that was rich in detail, much of which could be verified through research. Clearly Simmons, as Murphy, was in possession of special knowledge. She was able to mention places, people, and organizations that extensive research was able to verify had existed during her time.

Clearly there was a concentrated effort on part of the journalistic establishment to discredit the Bridey Murphy tale completely. They were assisted by many theologians who felt that Simmons was attacking the foundations of their religious beliefs. Many wanted the story destroyed by any means necessary. If the public could be convinced that Simmons, for whatever reason, was lying and that the story was a hoax, everything could return to normal.

But a dispassionate look at the evidence, while certainly not conclusive, is interesting. A skilled con artist who had time to prepare a story could, under hypnosis, have told the story that Simmons related. The key, however, is that there had been no preparation. And, much of the testimony was corroborated only after detailed and intensive research . . . which came about because of the clues provided by Simmons as Murphy.

In truth, what we have is a very interesting story, told by a woman who seems to be sincere and who was attacked for her participation in the "experiment." Much of what she said was corroborated . . . and much wasn't. The records that could answer some of the questions simply do not exist, either because of sloppy work, time, destruction, or inconvenience. In other words, there is no clear evidence that Simmons lied, that Bernstein was less than honest, or that the story is not true.

In the end, we each must decide what we want to believe. The only lesson to be learned from this episode is that those who have their own agenda are often less than honest in their criticisms. The clergyman undoubtedly believed that what he was writing was the truth, and if he stretched a point or two, it wasn't important. The end result justified his actions. Unfortunately, it leaves the rest of us in the cold, trying to guess which set of "facts" are accurate.

The germane question is the one that no one asked at the time and that was whether Bernstein's method of setting up the experiment, and his introduction of the idea of age regression beyond birth fatally damaged the results. Clearly he suggested to his subject that she could remember a time beyond her birth, and she did do that.

Does the evidence from the investigation outweigh that contamination, and is the contamination relevant? Those are questions that were never addressed.

All we can do, at this late date, is examine the evidence, all of it, and decide for ourselves. But we must remember that the evidence is tainted by the personal biases of those who are presenting it. We can hope that they are objective, but when they're not, there's not much we can do about it.

There may come a time, in the future, when questions like those raised around Bridey Murphy will be easy to answer. In today's environment, with the documentation that exists in government files, county records, computer data banks, and public libraries, it will be easy to verify data that a hundred years ago would have been obscure.

And it will be just as easy to construct a believable past based on the records and the documents that will exist. But maybe this is a question that can never be positively answered.

Twelve

Edgar Cayce and Reincarnation

The Search for Bridey Murphy had one other major ramification for those interested in the concept of reincarnation. In the book, Bernstein quoted heavily from the work of Edgar Cayce, a man who had become a champion of reincarnation, and who gave past life readings. Although Cayce was fairly well known because of his work in various areas of parapsychology, the Bridey Murphy case could have damaged his reputation and his work had the debunkers not been challenged by the Cayce group. Bridey Murphy did bring the readings of Cayce to the attention of many who had never heard of him or his work prior to the publication of the book.

Cayce was born on a farm outside of Hopkinsville, Kentucky on March 18, 1877 and died sixty-six years later, on January 3, 1945. He had little formal education but did learn to read and write, though he studied only one book and that was the Bible.

At twenty-one he was a salesman for a stationery company. While his career was beginning to blossom, Cayce was struck with a severe case of laryngitis and lost his voice. Medication failed to cure the problem, and doctors were unable to remedy it. Cayce was forced to quit his job as a salesman.

As a last resort, a traveling hypnotist placed Cayce in a trance in an attempt to cure him. Under the influence of hypnosis, Cayce was able to speak normally, but when he awakened, he was again mute. The traveling hypnotist left town, but a local amateur, Al Layne, wondered if he put Cayce under, and if Cayce could still speak under hypnosis, maybe Cayce could "explore" the problem himself. Under hypnosis Cayce might be able offer some sort of cure for his problem.

In the trance, Cayce was able to find the problem, and Layne, using a hypnotic suggestion offered a cure that might work. Cayce was to increase the blood flow to the damaged area. His neck turned pink and then crimson. After several minutes Cayce announced that the cure worked. He regained his voice.

Layne, after the success of the cure Cayce had devised for himself, wondered if the technique would work on others. Using hypnosis, Layne asked the "sleeping" Cayce how to remedy his own stomach trouble. Though Cayce knew nothing about medicine, he provided Layne with the proper information to cure himself.

Flush with that success, Layne wondered if Cayce's gift might not translate into a way of helping others. Cayce, who had absolutely no memory of what he said while under the influence of hypnosis, was reluctant to try. Layne convinced him to attempt a few more experiments. Cayce made it clear, however, that he would accept no money or any sort of payment for the advice he gave.

Cayce then embarked on a "career" that would produce more than fourteen thousand individual readings, providing medical advice and cures that had often evaded professionals. Each of the readings was duly recorded by a stenographer.

Experimentation continued, and Cayce learned that he did not have to be in the presence of the subject. Provided with a location and a time when the subject would be present, Cayce, under self-induced hypnosis, could examine the subject. Often, according to the notes taken, he provided detailed medical information to cure the ailment. Although it had not been Cayce's idea, he learned that if he probed more deeply into the subject's mind, he could uncover past lifetimes. These "life readings" eventually totaled about twenty-five hundred.

In one incredible case, Cayce told a man that he had lived as a Confederate soldier, providing the subject with a name and address of his former incarnation. Investigation revealed that a man who had lived at the address Cayce supplied had been a member of Robert E. Lee's Army of Northern Virginia and had served as a color sergeant.

In another case, outlined in detail in *Edgar Cayce on Reincarnation* by Noel Langley, Cayce told Patricia Farrier that she had lived and died near Fredericksburg, Virginia. He told Farrier and her sister that there were records available to corroborate the life reading.

The sisters traveled to Fredericksburg, and during the night, Emily was awakened as her sister struggled for breath. Unable to awaken Patricia, she called the hotel proprietor, and then a doctor. With difficulty they awakened Patricia. The sisters fled from Fredericksburg.

Cayce, in the life reading, learned that in her earlier life, Patricia had been playing in a root cellar filled with seedlings, cuttings, potatoes and herbs. While she was down there, a small earthquake caused the cellar to collapse, burying the young girl. She died of suffocation. Cayce believed that the hotel had been built either on the site of the root cellar, or close enough to it that it triggered an unconscious memory of that tragic event.

All of this is interesting, but it proves nothing to the skeptical. There are alternatives that can explain all the information—including coincidence. Other factors that might not have been recognized by the "controllers" including Layne, could account for Cayce's amazing success. Layne might have provided Cayce with nonverbal clues without realizing that he had done so. However, it is interesting that when corroboration was attempted, when facts could be checked, and when the old documents still existed, there seemed to be a high level of correlation.

There were doctors who had used Cayce's unique form of diagnosis. Surveys suggested that Cayce's rate of accuracy exceeded eighty percent and one doctor said that Cayce had never been wrong. What this meant, simply, was that some members of the medical profession recognized Cayce's ability to diagnose illness and disease and used it themselves. They might not have understood the process, but they had seen its positive results.

In fact, the October 9, 1910 edition of *The New York Times* reported on the unorthodox procedure of Dr. Wesley Ketchum, who had used Cayce to diagnose patients. From that moment, Cayce was bombarded with requests for assistance.

Bernstein, in *The Search for Bridey Murphy* recounts his search for the truth, writing that he not only interviewed doctors who had used

Cayce, but he had also interviewed the subjects of the readings, whether for medical reasons or for a general life reading.

Bernstein was impressed with what he found. There were dozens who swore that Cayce had helped them recover from injury, illness and disease. Others revealed that Cayce had been remarkably accurate in descriptions of their lives, providing answers to long-term questions for them.

In his book, Bernstein wrote, "But to me the most surprising aspect of our survey was the unexpectedly large number of sound, sensible individuals who accepted reincarnation with complete respect. While I was bashfully hiding behind terms like 'reincarnation stuff,' the people I interviewed were guilty of no such pussyfooting. To the contrary, they spoke out forcefully, with neither hesitation nor embarrassment, pointing out that careful thought would almost inevitably lead one to admit the possibility of this other dimension."

Noel Langley, in *Edgar Cayce on Reincarnation* writes that Cayce learned of this realm on August 10, 1923 when Arthur Lammers used Cayce's talents to confirm his beliefs in reincarnation. Cayce answered the questions in detail and when the session was over he was horrified to learn what he'd told Lammers. Reincarnation was not a topic that Cayce believed in and he felt, at that point, that his abilities were beginning to lead him in the wrong direction.

Although Cayce found this session at odds with his Christian beliefs, he continued to answer Lammers's questions. Cayce, after examining what he said in his "trance" state, believed that it neither challenged nor impugned the teachings of Christ. He believed that it underscored these teachings and "laid the foundations for a spiritual philosophy powerful enough to withstand the secular cynicism of this most turbulent of centuries."

Because of that, Cayce continued his "life readings" providing hundreds with an insight into their past lives which gave them solutions to present problems. Langley wrote about a man whose sister had obtained a life reading for him when he was only fourteen. While Cayce needed a location for the person so that he could "meet" for a medical diagnosis, he needed nothing of the sort for a "life reading."

Cayce was given the name of the subject, his birth date, the location of the birth and his parents. Cayce was then asked to provide the conditions of the present personality, as well as the names, locations and the relevant data of past lives that had helped shape the "entity" as it was called.

Cayce's reading of the entity provided a long and rich existence. Cayce and others suggest that not all lives manifested themselves in a reading, and that there was a group of "spirits" that are reincarnated frequently, as if trying for as much "life" experience as possible.

Cayce told of a life that spanned the reigns of Louis XIII and Louis XIV. As a man named Neil, he assisted the court as a "Master of the Robes." He dealt with fashion in the court and was responsible for the king's wardrobe. All this happened in the seventeenth century with a central date of about 1650.

In a life before that, he had lived on the Aegean coast of Greece. He was a tradesman named Colval. Colval was able, because it was the time of transition from one form of government to another, to obtain a position of power. According to Cayce, he abused his position and it did nothing to advance him spiritually.

Earlier still, he might have lived at the time of Alexander the Great and might have become a court physician. Even earlier, he was an Egyptian during one of the invasions. With all that data, it was possible for Cayce to identify the recurring factors encountered by the "entity."

The most controversial aspect of these life readings is Cayce's reference to the Lost Continent of Atlantis. Most historians and scholars believe that Atlantis was merely a myth created by the philosopher Plato, but Cayce provided a wealth of details about it.

It must be understood, that, according to

Cayce, the farther removed the event was from the present, the more difficult it was for him to "translate" his thoughts and impressions into the modern world. He could "observe" and understand what he was seeing, but it was sometimes nearly impossible to communicate it properly to those taking notes.

It was Cayce's interpretation that he was dealing with past life memories of Atlantis. For the boy, he reported that he had been named Amiaie-Oulieb, that he was an heir to the throne, and that he died by drowning as the last vestiges of Atlantis disappeared into the ocean.

Relating this to the present, Cayce suggested that the boy would find his "place" by seeking employment in a field that related to the clothing industry. It was suggested that he pay attention to his physical well-being.

The boy finally entered the job market and found his niche as a salesman, selling uniforms—such as band uniforms—to high schools. He did well, he was frequently promoted, and though he was the youngest salesman, he led them in sales.

During the Second World War, he was found to be 4F (unsuitable for military service), and the rationing of gas and restrictions on travel ended his career as a traveling salesman. He then worked in military clothing shops. When the war ended, he returned to his sales career.

Through life readings like this one, Cayce

and his followers developed a philosophy. It involved a "karma" in which the entity atoned in the present life for transgressions in the past. Neil, it seems, had indulged his gluttony while in the royal court in France. In his present life, he had a tender stomach that caused him to eat only bland foods. That was his "punishment" for his gluttony.

The readings by Cayce divided the karma into two categories; emotional karma and physical karma. Often manifestations of illness in one life time were the result of something committed in a previous life. The example used by Langley is the murderer in a past life who suffers from leukemia in this life. "A symbolic shedding of blood," according to Langley.

Jane Clephan, a college student, had an inferiority complex that was traceable, according to a Cayce reading, to a past life. She had been the wife of a doctor living in France who beat her and kept her at home, afraid of her beauty. He fought to keep her personality submerged.

In a still earlier life "the entity" of Jane Clephan had been persecuted during the time of Christ. Although a Christian, she had submerged her beliefs to avoid the rebuke of family and friends.

By examining these lives Cayce was able to tell the woman how to improve her current life. He suggested that she study music and that she work to overcome her feelings of inadequacy.

She had to heal herself in this life, but now she had an insight into her problems.

The soul, or entity, according to Cayce, had "traits" that passed from one life to the next. Those with a talent for music, were found to have lives that related, in some form or another to music. They might be a gifted piano player in one incarnation, a composer in another, and maybe a conductor in a third. Of course, the trait might skip a life as the entity tries something new.

The suggestion, then, is that by living a number of lives, a soul grows, reaching toward a state of perfection. The problems that plague a soul in one life help it reach that level between lives. A number of books about Cayce and his life are available for those who wish to understand more about the concepts of karma and life readings.

Cayce always tried to make it clear that his knowledge of reincarnation, and the concepts he was discussing were not at odds with Christian thought, but were complementary to it. Langley reconfirms the idea that all references to reincarnation have been eliminated from the Bible.

The problem for many is that there is no proof that reincarnation exists. They have a bias against it, reacting violently whenever it is discussed. They resort to inventing ridiculous explanations. Once these critics have labeled the phenomenon as paranormal, they are happy. With it labeled, whether properly or not, it can be dismissed.

One man, arguing against the idea of reincarnation, rejected the theories because one of those claiming a past life said that he had been born in 50 B.C. The man said that if you were born in 50 B.C., you couldn't have known it because the calendar counting the years that referred to the time before Christ as B.C. didn't exist until after the reincarnated man would have died in that lifetime.

Of course, it could be argued that the person being interviewed is a modern individual, able to translate past information into modern terminology. It could be argued that a person who claims to be foreign in a past life but who can still speak English is able to translate the foreign language at some unconscious level. Knowledge from today does not desert the mind as the person is regressed.

Or, it could be argued that the man who said he was born in 50 B.C. was lying, trying to make a name for himself on the lecture circuit or to impress his friends. But, because one man possibly lied about his memories does not negate the stories of reincarnation by others.

The problem is that the concept cannot be verified by independent corroboration. We can check into facts provided, but that doesn't prove that reincarnation is real. It proves that the facts are accurate. It might not be easy to explain how the subject knew those facts because they are quite obscure. But, if they can be found in the research, then that information, no matter how obscure, was available to everyone including the one claiming reincarnation.

It must be remembered that we might not be able to explain how the subject learned the data. There might be that some other reasonable explanation, one that we haven't thought of as completely reasonable.

Bridey Murphy had information that required days of research in obscure books held in libraries in a foreign country. No evidence was ever presented that she had traveled to Ireland, that she had been in communication with the library, or that anyone she knew had done the research. Clearly she was in possession of data that an average American woman born in Wisconsin and living in Colorado would not normally have had. Just as clearly, her descriptions of her previous life in Ireland could be verified, to a certain extent.

Does this, by itself, prove that reincarnation is a fact? No. It provides us with some interesting information that is not easily explainable in contemporary terms.

Reincarnation, as outlined by Cayce, is a fascinating phenomenon. There seems to be some positive evidence suggesting that it is real. But proof is lacking and maybe that is the way it's supposed to be. If we knew the truth, then maybe we'd just give up when life became tough, figuring we'd just come back later, when life is easier. We could punch out of this life, hoping that in the next one we would make better choices.

Thirteen

Archaeology a New Way

If reincarnation exists, it can become a way of searching the past. Archaeology is a study of the past of the human race. It seems natural that a combination of the two would yield data that would be valuable in both arenas but might be available to either separately. In archaeology there are always questions that can't be answered simply because we are too separated from our ancient past. Written records and oral traditions only supply so much data.

But . . . if we could tap into the wealth of information that lies just beyond the surface of the mind, and if that information was accurate, then the benefits for understanding the past would be overwhelming.

Almost none of those engaging in past life regression have tapped into this as a source of archaeological data. Little effort has been made to corroborate the data gathered in past life regressions simply because that is not the purpose of those regressions. The notable exception is Bridey Murphy. She was a "resident" of the mid-nineteenth century and there was little that happened in that time frame that hasn't been effectively communicated or documented.

There are, however, hundreds who claim past lives during the Dark Ages, the Roman Empire, in ancient Greece and Egypt and even beyond that. These are interesting stories that might provide us of the modern world a glimpse into what it was actually like for our ancestors in their ancient worlds.

Edgar Cayce, in his life readings, supplied people with information he received about their past lives. Many of them had lived in the recent past while others gained information that went back into the far distant past. Cayce could, therefore, provide answers about past lives that seemed to intrude into the modern world.

Ruth Montgomery reports in *Here and Hereafter*, that a young man living in Norfolk, Virginia had been, almost from birth, interested in war. He maneuvered his blocks as if they were tanks, and when he could speak, he began to shout, "Heil Hitler." When he could read, he devoured books about the Nazis and their leadership, and even sickened his mother with a description of a death camp.

According to Montgomery, a life reading by a psychic was made for the youth. It was determined that he had been a German soldier who had been killed during the World War II. He kept up his "militaristic" attitudes until he was almost old enough for the draft. At that time, he changed his mind, deciding that Hitler had been a fool.

Questioning of the boy could have, if handled properly, provided inside information into the operation of those German units the boy claimed, or rather the psychic claimed, he had been a member of. It might have provided some corroboration for the theories of reincarnation if the boy's descriptions had been accurate. It would be a way of testing the data against the memories of people who lived through that time. It would have been an interesting experiment had it been attempted early enough in the boy's life.

If it could be established that such memories were accurate, then a precedent would be set. If a boy who could not possibly have served in the World War II German Army could describe its inner workings to the satisfaction to those who had actually served, then the memories, regardless of the source, could be used to understand our history.

Unfortunately, such was not the case. The boy's mother was concerned about his attitudes and his rebellious nature. She would do nothing to encourage his interest in that era and she can't be faulted for that.

Another researcher found a young woman who was interested in the Union forces during the Civil War—specific regiments from New York. She gathered and read everything she could about them, talked knowledgeably about them and details of their drills, and even knew the procedures for loading and firing the percussion-cap rifles and revolvers used during that time.

Studying specific regiments and their activities during the Civil War is not that unusual. But the girl seemed to know more about it than one would have expected. A life reading revealed that as a young Civil War (male) soldier she had fought with two different New York regiments and then been killed just as the war was winding down.

There are those who study the Civil War, joining modern regiments that are formed specifically to "reenact" that period of history. They live as if they are fighting the Civil War, camp out, drill, and study the campaigns carefully. They know every detail about who served and when, what battles the regiment fought, and if and how they were deactivated after the war.

The information was there for anyone who wanted to search it out. Again, if the young woman was right about the things she said, then another level of credibility has been established. And, again, with that information available, the study would prove nothing other than she seemed to possess information she ordinarily wouldn't have had.

Melody Anderson mentioned lives as a pioneer woman in the nineteenth century and as an American Indian woman, at another time. She mentioned the clothing and the shoes she wore. A little research showed that the details were accurate.

A pattern had been established. There are people in possession of historical information far out of proportion to that normally available to the average person. So, the question of interest becomes whether anyone can remember a past life that reaches back before recorded time. Anderson said that she had spoken to one such woman who seemed to have flashed on an existence that was over a hundred thousand years old.

Anderson said, "I think of one woman in particular . . . I did a workshop . . . I was doing a class and I was going to do a sample of a past life regression . . . It was an all-woman workshop . . . This woman regressed into what was obviously a very, very primitive, extremely primitive, pre-history experience. She was a masculine embodiment . . . and she was so masculine . . . so Neanderthal [used to describe the primitive condition rather than an accurate description of the time frame] if you would . . . without a doubt. Her voice, her language, the volume in her throat was so masculine, so big, so overpowering . . . it was so funny to watch them . . . all the women kind of shifted, kind of inched over so they were all on the other side of the room . . . Like they could not get away from this person fast enough.

". . . now as I recall because I didn't write this one down, she was very disregarding of what is feminine, and very warrior-like . . . I'm trying to remember what her lesson was in that . . . Well, that's what it was. It was about embracing . . . she was one who did not embrace her masculine very well . . . In the balance of it she was one who had an attitude about what it was to be masculine . . . For her to experience that pure, raw masculine was quite an experience for her."

Anderson also said that Edgar Cayce was able to describe a vaulted room under the Sphinx in Egypt. Inside, according to Cayce, is a record of a prehistorical civilization that will change our whole concept of what is historical. Anderson said that just two years ago scientists and archaeologists determined there is a square area underneath the Sphinx that could be the vault described by Cayce.

If this turns out to be an accurate prediction by Cayce, then it demonstrates that there is some reliability to the gathering of data in such a bizarre fashion. It suggests that archaeologists might have a new tool and that those who study the history of the human race might have a new weapon in their arsenal.

This can be taken even further, for almost anyone who delves into reincarnation runs up against the legend of Atlantis. Cayce spoke at length about Atlantis. Melody Anderson mentioned it many times. There are strong connections between reincarnation and the lost continent of Atlantis.

Cayce, in his life readings, discovered many who had been residents of Atlantis, some of them having reincarnated on the lost continent a couple of times. Cayce believed that Atlantis was the first place that the human race inhabited, over ten million years ago, long before the human race is believed to have evolved, according to modern science.

Cayce mentioned three eras that were marked by cataclysms that finally destroyed Atlantis. Cayce never reported when the first disaster struck, but he marked the second at 28,000 B.C. and the final one in 9600 B.C. That was the one that Plato wrote about in the *Timaeus*.

Plato claims the story of Atlantis came from an Egyptian priest who had told it to the Greek statesman Solon. Writing from the viewpoint of the priest, Plato related:

Many great and wonderful deeds are recorded of your State in our histories; but one of them exceeds all the rest in greatness and valor; for these histories tell of a mighty power which was aggressing wantonly against the whole of Europe and Asia, and to which your city put an end. The power came forth out of the Atlantic Ocean, for in those days the Atlantic was navigable; and there was an island situated in front of the straits which you call the Columns of Heracles: the island was larger than Libya and Asia put together and was the way to other islands, and from the islands you might pass through the whole of the opposite continent which surrounded the true ocean; for this sea which is within the Straits of Heracles is only a harbor, having a narrow entrance, but that other is a real sea, and the surrounding land may be most truly called a continent.

Now, in the island of Atlantis there was a great and wonderful empire, which had rule over parts of the continent: and, besides these, they subjected the parts of Libya within the Columns of Heracles as far as Egypt, and of Europe as far as Tyrrhenia. The vast power thus gathered into one, endeavored to subdue at one blow our country and yours, and the whole of the land which was within the straits; and then, Solon, your country was shone forth, in the excellence of her virtue and

198 *Kevin D. Randle*

strength, among all mankind; for she was
the first in courage and military skill, and
was the leader of the Hellenes. And when
the rest fell off from her, being compelled
to stand alone, after having undergone the
extremity of danger, she defeated and tri-
umphed over the invaders, and preserved
from slavery those who were not yet subjected, and freely liberated all the others
who dwelt within the limits of Heracles.
But afterward there occurred violent
earthquakes and floods, and in a single
day and night of rain all your warlike men
in a body sank into the earth, and the island of Atlantis in like manner disappeared, and was sunk beneath the sea,
which in those parts is impassible and im-
penetrable, because there is such a quan-
tity of shallow mud in the water; and this
was caused by the subsidence of the island.

Cayce claimed that the lost continent lay on
the ocean floor in the area of Bimini in the
Bahamas. He believed parts of it would rise
again in 1968 or 1969. Although nothing spec-
tacular was found, in 1968 stone formations
that to some extent suggested the bases of pyramids, roads and walls were found in the ocean
near Bimini. A few people suggested these
were the first of the ruins of Atlantis to surface.
Many scholars have believed that the legend

of Atlantis is nothing more than a fiction invented by Plato. Even his contemporaries believed it was nothing more than a fairy tale.

Others believed it to be the truth. Ignatius Donnelly, a U.S. congressman, published *Atlantis: The Antediluvian World*. Donnelly claimed that many of the similarities between the Old and New World could be explained by the people of Atlantis. He thought that the pyramids of Egypt and the pyramids of Central and South America had a common root and that root was firmly embedded in Atlantis.

Donnelly's theories, however, do not conform to modern archaeological thought. The pyramid shape, for example, is simple enough that it is reasonable to assume that two separate cultures could develop it independently. And, as archaeologists point out, the Egyptian pyramids were built as tombs for kings while those in Central America were built as platforms for temples. Though some burial has been discovered inside the Meso-American pyramids, that seems to be incidental to the causes of construction rather than a reason for it.

From a scientific, archaeological, and research standpoint, there is no solid evidence that Atlantis was ever anything more than a myth. However, in the late nineteenth century, the archaeological thought was that Troy never existed, and the story of Helen, Achilles, and the Trojan War were figments of Homer's imagination. It wasn't until the remains of a series of cities were found on the location that marked Troy that scientists became to accept that Homer's writings, though embellished, reported on actual events and locations of ancient Greece in his time.

This does not mean that Atlantis existed outside the minds of various people. It merely points out that not all the data are in, and that an open mind should be kept.

Rosemary Ellen Guiley, like many others, claims that the souls of those who lived in Atlantis have been reincarnated and therefore, "interviewed." Writing in *Tales of Reincarnation,* she explains that many of those who were in Atlantis have chosen the twentieth century in which to return. Maybe it is because many of the wonders we admire today are those that supposedly graced Atlantis. Maybe there is a resonance with our civilization because of its use of technology.

Guiley quoted a number of sources, saying that many had believed, at first, they were in the classical Roman or Greek settings. They wore white clothing, saw white marble and white structures. There were columned temples and buildings, as well as pyramids which according to Guiley, were structures for focusing power. There are tales of aviation, but not the system that marks our world. These are small, individual craft that float through the air carrying a single passenger.

Dick Sutphen, who wrote *Past Lives, Future Lives*, said that his former wife, Trenna, had known him when both were philosophy students in Atlantis. They finished their studies, were married and then went into the field to promote education. During a return trip to their school, a prophet warned them of the disaster about to strike Atlantis. Before they could leave, the city was hit by a tidal wave. They opted to join the spiritual plane.

Disaster struck Atlantis because of the corruption that seeped into it. The enlightened Atlanteans lost sight of what was right and were destroyed. Maybe it was the misuse of technology that caused their destruction.

Melody Anderson remembers Atlantis in a "spiritual" state and recalls little of the technology. There was transparent material in the windows but she doesn't know if it was glass as we know it. She recalls a woman who used stones and crystals as a way to telepathically communicate with others. This woman felt bad because one of the messages had been garbled and there were severe consequences for it.

Anderson's focus was not to learn about the technology of Atlantis, but to understand the spiritual aspects of it. She has little information about everyday life in Atlantis.

She does mention that a number of people

she's regressed mentioned jewelry that seems to be some kind of badge of rank. The position of a person in the community is related to the necklace and the symbols on it. Hers was a sphere on a necklace with a crescent shape suspended under it like the smile on a happy face.

There are questions that rational and skeptical minds will ask. If Atlantis existed, why is there no tangible evidence for it? If Atlanteans had obtained a level of technological sophistication, why are all traces of their civilization gone? Why don't the ancient records of Egypt, Greece, and Rome reflect some kind of trade with Atlantis? According to those who claim past lives in Atlantis, Atlanteans had the means to travel great distances. There should be some archaeological evidence of contact between those ancient civilizations around the Mediterranean Sea and Atlantis, but there seems to be nothing in the archæological record.

These are fair questions that might have no solid answers. We can speculate. First, there is the possibility that the Atlanteans were not as technologically advanced as we like to think. If such is the case, then the means to travel great distances may have been no more available to them than to the Egyptians.

If Cayce is right, and Atlantis sank into the sea in 9600 B.C., that means it disappeared more than eleven thousand years ago. Our written history doesn't record events that old.

There are hints of great floods, and Atlantis certainly experienced a great flood. Maybe that is where some of the tradition for stories of a great flood came from.

If those who claim Atlantean lives are correct, the sorts of technological artifacts that we could use to prove it simply do not exist and never have, in our society. If they built their cities of stone, then all we would find are the processed stone but nothing to suggest an age for when it was quarried.

But if those claiming Atlantean connections are right, and Atlantis existed, then we are missing out on a good source of data. Through past-life regression, we could learn the location of Atlantis, we could learn about the everyday life of the people who lived on Atlantis, we could tap into the technology that let their civilization flourish and possibly adapt it to our own use.

This is a question that needs to be addressed by those with the credentials to explore it, but as is the case with so many of the ancient wonders, we are reluctant to drop our veil of sophistication to admit that such things might be true. No scientist wants to admit that he is studying life in Atlantis because of the reaction of his colleagues.

But what about acupuncture? When first reintroduced to the western world in the 1960s, almost no one believed in it. How could sticking needles into the body alleviate aches and pains? Somehow it does.

Rather than rejecting this notion of Atlantis out of hand because it requires an acceptance of reincarnation, it should be studied, by means of legitimate studies designed to test the data, to learn if they are accurate—not studies designed to debunk . . . and not studies designed to prove. Rather, there should be impartial, scientific research to discover if there is any validity to reincarnation, Atlantis, and archaeological investigation using the tools of past life regression to learn the truth.

Fourteen

A Guide for Past-Life Regressions

Hypnosis is not necessary for tapping into a past life. Hypnosis is a tool used by those who engage in past-life regressions because it allows the subject to focus his or her attention. But hypnosis, as a tool, can be misapplied, allowing the hypnotist to control the situation and create testimony. The suggestion that someone has lived before can be easily introduced into a session, and in the case of past-life readings, the suggestion is often made before the subject is regressed. In other words, it is a process that is easily contaminated by even the most conscientious hypnotist.

Melody Anderson, of Ruidoso, New Mexico, now an expert in past-life regression, offers workshops and classes. She uses hypnosis, but also relies on techniques she learned in *A Practical Guide to Past Life Regression* by Florence Wagner McClain, and that she developed during her own work. Anderson makes it clear that hypnosis is not a necessary component of a past-life regression but allows a past life to be more easily accessed.

According to Anderson, "It is so incredibly simple . . . The first time I did it before I was trained, I bought a book and gave it to my . . . friend and said read this to me. I wanted to experience a past life and I probably experienced one of the most profound past lives that I have ever experienced. It scared . . . her . . . she went home and said, 'Don't you ever ask me to do that again.' "

That was the result of an exercise that she read in the book. It is a simple exercise, not unlike self-hypnosis. The subject is required to get into a comfortable position away from distractions and outside noise. Then, starting with the scalp, the person is told to relax, concentrating first on the top of the head and moving down the body in slow stages until the feet and toes are reached. If there is a problem, or the subject begins to tense up, then part of the exercise is repeated.

Next, the subject starts with the feet and tries to eliminate feeling from them. The idea is to separate the conscious mind from physical knowledge of the body. The process continues on up, as the subject tries to forget about the body. If he or she has trouble, then pretense is substituted. The point is to move on, even if part of the exercise seems to fail. It is more important to create a state of mind rather than an actual, physical sensation of being separated.

For those initiated into hypnotic technique, the relaxation exercise is familiar and easily understood. The point of the separating the mind from the body is to disassociate the "spirit" from the physical world. It is an attempt to create a mood for an out-of-body experience because the next step is to "see" yourself outside the house or apartment, looking back at it and describing it in detail as if outside looking back.

This serves to further create the proper environment, and to focus attention on a specific task that shouldn't fail. Nearly everyone can describe, with a great deal of accuracy, the exterior of the house or apartment. The exercise also creates a mood where the subject is not required to have an out-of-body experience, but a simulation of the event. Again, it is all part of a created environment where the subject feels comfortable with the exercise.

Once the subject is relaxed and has progressed through the exercises, he or she is ready for the next step. Now the situation is set so that it simulates a near-death experience. The "controller" describes a scene to the subject. Slowly counting, and mixing in the description of a long dark tunnel with light at the end, the controller takes the subject from the entrance and out into the light, explaining all the time that as it becomes brighter that the subject is passing from the current lifetime into the past. Through the tunnel is the passage to another life somewhere in the past. The suggestion is that the subject is moving, mentally, back through time. That the past is becoming more real and that it can be seen as if it was only a few days earlier.

And when the count reaches one, the subject is now in a previous life-time. The controller then pauses, and asks that the subject begin to look around to see what is happening. The controller asks questions such as what the subject has on his or her feet, the type of clothing being worn, whether the subject is male or female and what year it is.

Once that has been established, it's possible to leap forward in that past life-time so that the subject can see what is happening five years after the initial event. The same questions used earlier can provide more detail about the life being viewed.

If the controller wants, it is possible to explore other life-times. When ready, the controller suggests that it is possible to see into a previous life. The same techniques provide data about that life-time.

Anderson, using the technique, with no formal training at the time, and with her friend's help, was able to experience a past life-time.

She said, "I was an Indian woman . . . first a young woman . . . my first experience was walking up a mountain and it was cold, it was just freezing cold outside and I was just fascinated by my clothing because even while I was in the trance I'm sitting there thinking, I didn't know Indians dressed like this . . . I'm walking up the hill because it's not the regular Indians like from John Wayne movies, I'm walking up this mountain and it's cold and it's snowing and I am so freezing and I'm shaking and I remember I was so cold that my whole body was moving . . . after I realized that I was alone and I was totally alone and I just started crying and I was freezing and I was miserable . . . so she progressed me forward in time and I had realized that I was without my community and I was never clear on that and I had lost my tribe. I was alone so I was just wandering through the woods. She progressed and I found myself in this community . . . Indian community . . . found myself fascinated by the teepees because they were much larger than I had imagined and they had a floor and I remember that it had a floor to it. I had expected that when I stepped into it—I had expected it to have the ground and I saw myself later in life as a kind of "auntie" to the children . . . I was a kind of teacher and . . . my last images is a kind of "ring around the rosie" type game for the children there. A sense that I had had a time of struggle and I knew what it was to be alone and have nowhere to go . . . I was finally able to find my place and to belong . . . to be loved and accepted . . . It was a message that was pertinent at that time. It had a lot of meaning for me there . . ."

Anderson, because of her work, believes that these glimpses are of her past lives. She calls the technique "induction [or] what we understand to be hypnosis. What I call it is just an expanded state of consciousness."

She is also quick to point out that her work "from a scientific viewpoint . . . would be polluted." She is saying that she introduces the idea of reincarnation to the subject, or the subject has come to her for a past-life reading already aware of what will happen. The possibility of reincarnation already exists in the mind of the subject. There is almost no way to design an experiment to get at a past-life reading without some measure of leading and contamination according to Anderson.

Her purpose is not to produce good science, but to provide insights for those who are having troubles in this life. Anderson says that many problems we experience are the result of a trauma or event in a past life. By understanding that, as a root cause, the trouble of today can be eliminated.

As an example, she said, "My own personal experience is that I have a father and it just makes him crazy that I do not get a real job. And just forever and ever that I was always so angry about it, why don't you just accept it until I did a regression in which I was back in the frontier land here and again in my work it doesn't occur to me to ask, but out West somewhere and wearing this long skirt out West. I have a little boy who's about ten years old walking with me and I have these bundles with me. Apparently I'm a dressmaker. I'm widowed and am just making ends meet as a dressmaker and I'm walking across a street and I get run over . . . a wagon out of control. I died and my little boy ten years old and I have made no arrangements for him . . . no provision whatsoever. He's [an orphan] with nothing. Nothing. Apparently there is no "great" people there . . . a family does take him in but he lives in a barn and he doesn't get to go to school because they just work the heck out of him. So they work him like a slave, basically, and all he does is get fed and barely a roof over his head. Well, I realized that was my father . . . and what that does for me is give me a compassion that when I deal with him and I hear that fear in his voice now I talk to him so differently . . . I don't say get off my back . . trust me . . . I know this must be tough."

She believed this happened in the late nineteenth century but said, "See, that's the thing. My problem is that I don't get specific . . . I just get the picture, the image and the emotion . . . I'm real good about what I'm wearing . . . I was dressed like an Indian once and I remember being so incredibly fascinated about my shoes because I had never seen shoes like that . . ."

Anderson said that she had done little work in an attempt to verify what she is told: ". . . my motivation is very different. My motivation is towards healing and so I don't ask names, dates and what was the name of the street and that sort of thing. What I'm focusing on is how are you feeling."

And though she hasn't been motivated, according to her, ". . . there have been times when people have been incredibly specific. Now this has been a time in which I did a regression . . . I regressed myself and I was so stunned that I went out bought this ancient history book and was able to do some confirmation . . . about Alexandria and a life . . . at that time I didn't know there was an Alexandria, and there was a great library . . . The only thing I know was that I was in the library and nobody there liked me . . .

There are problems with the technique, however. Anderson said, "A guy that I regressed just the other day experienced . . . he had all these things going on in his life . . . like everything he was reading and he just kept hearing a lot of stuff about Jews. He was thinking why is it all of the sudden? I'm not Jewish and why is it that all the people I happen to be reading are Jewish . . . What are these coincidences about? So he makes an appointment with me and says "Let's kind of look at this." Was I a Jew or what was it.

"He accessed it and he was part of the SS . . . and as soon as he saw himself in this uniform, he just started crying and thinking, 'Gosh . . .' As he began to go through the experiences and he found that he was a transportation manager in charge of making sure the trains ran and transported them from one place to another."

The thoughts that come immediately to mind is that this is a younger man. From the detail provided, he was obviously some kind of Nazi transportation officer during World War II. At least that would be the conclusion if the discussion centered on reincarnation.

But that didn't seem to be the case. Anderson said, "The man who so vividly did all of this, talked about it and went through the emotions and the forgiveness and the compassion and everything . . . afterwards, when we're talking and this experience is over . . . he died . . . in this experience . . . he died two years after he was born as the man today. So that's what I'm saying. What do you make of it? Obviously science goes right out the window, right?

"What I make of it is that he has within his unconscious . . . call it genetic memory or whatever about that era and that he was able to access it because what he . . . the healing that came from him was about compassion and about knowing that there are some things that it's not enough for me to work for my own self benefit . . . that my actions . . . to recognize how my actions impact others and that I have a responsibility to the society. So what does he do? He accesses a past life in which he had no regard for anybody than anybody else and the fact he had this great car, great title and he made a ton of money and people feared him.

"This one, this experience clearly, was not an actual, legitimate past-life experience. Was it healing? You're damned right. It was more healing than anything he'd done before then.

"The thing is, I used that same technique for him to experience that—as for someone else to experience something else. . . and going to look in the books and found this checks out and this checks out . . . and they were still very emotional, they were still extremely vivid . . . to the patch on his sleeve and his mother's re-action to him and it was very emotional. It's one of those things that if it wasn't for the date, he would have sworn it was true."

Does this negate the past-life regression? No. There may be, as Anderson suggested, other factors involved. She believes that there is a higher consciousness and it is possible that the man tapped into that in some fashion.

Of course, the other problem is the date of the transportation officer's death. The man believed that he had died as the SS man two years after he had been born into his current life. But that was based on his knowledge of the World War II and the events of the 1940s. If he was wrong about that, then the information does nothing to disprove the concept of reincarnation.

Or, it might be that the man had another experience earlier in his life that had been repressed and manifested itself in this sort of an experience. The technique used was to probe the mind, and it's possible that the mind produced this "skewed" view of his world.

This problem, manifesting itself in one man does nothing to suggest that other, similar experiences are not real. It might suggest, however, that the techniques are open to outside influences and can be contaminated in some fashion.

The whole problem is one of interpretation and it is up to each "controller," and each "subject" to interpret the results of a regression. There are no hard and fast rules. Conventional science does not recognize past-life regression, preferring to ignore it. That doesn't mean that the scientific attitude is wrong or that such things do not exist.

However, for those wanting to do scientific research, the problem here is the same as that for study of the near-death experience. How do you design a set of experiments to test reincarnation? Every objective test is contaminated in the beginning.

The guidelines here, however, will provide some useful information to those who would like to explore reincarnation on their own. Caution should be exercised any time such an undertaking is attempted. The human mind is still an unknown area to science. As Anderson said about the mind, "The more I study it the more I learn about it, the more I know that we don't know diddle."

Part IV: Conclusions

Fifteen

The Near-Death Experience and Reincarnation

The question that can be asked is how does the concept of reincarnation relate to near-death experiences? Are they related somehow, or are they two separate and distinct areas of the paranormal?

The first and easiest answer is to point out that very few trained researchers are investigating reincarnation. It is left, for the most part, to amateurs. A few psychologists have attempted to study it, but that is the exception rather than the rule.

By contrast, there are many doctors, psychologists, and trained researchers studying the idea of a near-death experience. Almost everyone admits the phenomenon exists. It is the interpretation of that experience that is open to debate. As mentioned earlier, some of these researchers believe there are mundane, physical explanations for near death, while others believe that it is a legitimate glimpse of what happens on the other side.

One of the elements reported by those claiming a past life is the death experience not unlike the NDE. The near-death phenomenon only recently has been reported. Raymond Moody alerted the world to the NDE in his 1975 book, *Life After Life*. Even then, it was not widely reported and investigated until the 1980s. Those who report NDEs do not necessarily believe in reincarnation, and in fact, some of them reject the whole idea of reincarnation out of hand. As one man said, "Once is more than enough."

There have been many who have reported a theory of reincarnation, the most famous of these are Edgar Cayce and Morey Bernstein. Their stories, because they preceded the NDE phenomenon, might provide some insight into this relationship. It cannot be claimed that those reporting reincarnation were contaminated by the data about the near-death experience because it simply did not exist then.

A careful reading of the Bridey Murphy story demonstrates this connection between NDEs and reincarnation. Murphy, in the course of the experiment conducted by Morey Bernstein was able to accurately describe her death. He was surprised by this, assuming, wrongly, that once she was dead, her perception in this world would cease. However, according to Murphy, she left her body and watched the scene inside the house after she died. According to Murphy, "I stayed in my house . . . stayed there with Brian [her husband]."

Bernstein questioned her about the activities long after her death. She talked of being "ditched" which, according to later research was a method of burial used in Ireland at that time. She did, periodically, try to talk to her husband, but "he wouldn't listen."

Her out-of-body experience lasted "for years." She remained in the house, watching as Brian played out his life. She also traveled "home to Cork" to visit her brother, Duncan. She was surprised that he was so old. She, of course, hadn't seen Duncan for a number of years.

It is interesting that Murphy talked about her death in terms of what happened after she died. But Melody Anderson reports that almost everyone she regresses goes through a death experience. "I simply say, 'Once the body is still, where do you go? What do you do?'"

She said, "Generally they report they rise above it . . . A guy . . . last week said that he stayed for quite a long time [in the area where he had died]." He had remained at the scene of his death, watching everything that had gone on around him.

In the near-death experience, the subject frequently mentions that he or she is no longer part of the scene. They have risen above it, and are looking down on it and watching it as if it is something happening to someone else. They witness the situation as if separated from it just as Bridey Murphy suggested, and as Melody Anderson reported.

Betty Eadie, in *Embraced by the Light,* not only looked down on the situation, but "journeyed" home to see what her husband and children were doing at the hour of her death. Since she returned to the living a few hours later, she didn't have an opportunity to spend "years" watching her family grow older as Murphy reported she did.

What this means, simply, is that those who claim reincarnation and those who claim a near-death experience, do report similar activities after their deaths. Murphy had an out-of-body experience, as do many of those who have NDEs such as Betty Eadie. The major difference is that Murphy didn't return to the body she left but was reincarnated, or rather, born, into the body of Ruth Simmons many years later. Eadie came back to the body she had left, according to her, a couple of hours earlier.

Another aspect of the NDE phenomenon, is the idea that those who have just died are met by relatives who are long dead, or that they see Jesus or God. Sometimes they refer to it as a "God-presence" or a "God-energy."

Melody Anderson said, "I've had people report . . . a meeting with Christ or God . . . or an angel . . . it depends on how they term it."

In *Children of the Light* Melvin Morse reports that "Katie" told of two women who took her to meet the Heavenly Father and Jesus. She was asked if she wanted to go home, but told the Heavenly Father she wanted to stay. Jesus asked if she wanted to see her family again and she said, "Yes." With that, she awakened in the hospital.

In *Is There Life After Life,* Jonathan Cott reports that Tom Sawyer, a heavy equipment operator told a "20/20" audience that, "My heart stopped . . . then before me was the most magnificent light; it's The Light in capital letters, and it's . . . the essence of God."

Bridey Murphy reported that she met with her little brother who had died in infancy so many years earlier. She had to tell him who she was because, according to Bernstein, "Presumably the baby would not have recognized this sixty-six-year-old woman; and she had to tell him who she was. On the other hand, Bridey recognized him at once . . ."

So there is a parallel there as well. Moody writes about meeting others . . . or the being of light. This has been reported by those claiming reincarnation, though Anderson did say that she had not had anyone tell her specifically about seeing the bright light which is a major part of the near death experience. With the new interest in near death, and Anderson's study of reincarnation, she had been looking for that aspect of it to be revealed.

However, while reviewing another aspect of the near-death phenomenon as it relates to the theories of reincarnation, Anderson did say, "I've had it reported where they've gone through almost like a vortex . . . a lifting . . . one of them specifically talked about a vortex."

This could easily be the tunnel that many of those have mentioned in their near-death experiences. Some have mentioned that they have felt drawn into the tunnel, sucked into it as if something was pulling them along. There is no real light, just the feeling of being inside a tunnel.

Moody reports in *Life After Life* that one of his informants said, "The first thing that happened—it was real quick—was that I went through this dark, black vacuum at super speed."

Another said, "I was in an utterly back, dark void. It was very difficult to explain, but I felt as if I was moving through in a vacuum . . ."

The connection could be as simple as the word choice by either the researchers or the subjects. A vortex can be described as a spinning, black tunnel. A tornado is a funnel cloud that touches the ground, sucking everything into it. It is, in essence, a vortex. Viewed another way, it is a tunnel, small or narrow at one end, and wide at the far end.

Moody also reports that there is a review of the life experience by many who claim a near-death experience. Anderson maintains that the time between one life and another is used for a reflection on what happened during the just-completed incarnation. It is a slow review of what has happened to the person during life.

There are other areas where the two experiences coincide. Those who have a near-death experience claim that their outlook on death is changed. They no longer fear the prospect but are looking forward to it as one would antici-pate a vacation in the summer.

Anderson said that her past-life regressions had had similar effects on her. She is not con-cerned about death because of what she has seen and learned during past-life regressions. All of it had a soothing, relaxing affect on her, not unlike those claimed by others who have had a near-death experience.

Many past-life memories are triggered spon-taneously. Something seen, felt, smelled, pro-duces a strong memory in the person. A scene of the past flashed in front of them, producing a feeling not unlike déjà vu. Often they can see a scene superimposed on the city or room around them, playing out like a television pro-gram. They might not have had any thoughts of reincarnation or past lives until that one strange and unexplainable event.

The NDE is sometimes masked in a similar way, hidden from the conscious mind. Once they have regained consciousness, they don't remember a thing about what they saw. It is only later that something triggers that specific memory.

Gilles Bedard wrote in *McLean's:* "I didn't remember the experience at that time. But a month after I left the hospital, I had another one. During the night, I had a sensation of falling into a tunnel. Going into it I knew I was about to die, but just before arriving at the end of the tunnel, I woke up . . . And it was then that I remembered the earlier experience."

One of the major, and interesting areas of overlap is corroboration. Moody writes that those experiencing near-death can often tell those who were in the emergency room, operating room, or hospital rooms, what was happening while they were unconscious and probably dead. This tends to corroborate the stories of near-death. These are facts that can be checked. These do not lead directly to the conclusion that near-death is a glimpse of the afterlife, but it is information that can be confirmed by the researchers.

With reincarnation there can be some corroboration. William Barker, on assignment from the *Denver Post,* attempted to corroborate portions of the Bridey Murphy story with some success. Again, this was not absolute proof that Murphy had been reincarnated as Ruth Simmons, but it did suggest some very interesting questions.

Edgar Cayce, during his past-life readings, provided those with incarnations in the recent past, meaning the nineteenth century, with the information they could use to corroborate their past lives. Many of them were able to learn who they had been in previous lives and how they had died.

Anderson said that she didn't bother with that because, to her, it wasn't important. She believed in past life and she knew, from a scientific point of view, her work was contaminated. For it to be successful, she needed to ask questions that made it impossible for her to do corroborative research. Besides, according to Anderson, that was not the point of her work. If others, such as those regressed, had the desire to learn more about their specific past lives, then that was up to them to pursue the search.

The point here, is to demonstrate that the two phenomena are linked through common experience. In one case, the subject is returned into the present life, and in the other, the subject is talking about something that happened in the distant past.

Both can provide us with new clues as to

what happens after we die. There is a growing body of information about NDE and reincarnation. Independent research is being done by men and women searching for answers.

There is, however, one major difference and that is the level of the training of those conducting research. The public, and the media, are ready to believe what the doctors who study NDE have to say. Journalists look at this, interview doctors on both sides and report it to the public. Both sides of this controversy are treated with respect because both sides have degrees and training and are seen as qualified experts. To journalists the message isn't as important as the people delivering it.

Those searching for evidence of reincarnation may be as well trained in their specific fields but the theories they express are too radical to be accepted. We are left with platitudes, such as: extraordinary claims require extraordinary proof. This doesn't answer questions but allows people to reject the claims without having to think about them.

But there is a body of evidence that suggests there is something to reincarnation. The adverse reaction by some to the story of Bridey Murphy makes no sense. She was either telling the truth or it was a hoax. If she was telling the truth, that didn't prove that she had been reincarnated as Ruth Simmons but it did suggest something strange was happening to her.

Rather than investigate, the story is wrongly attacked, labeled, and then rejected out of hand. Most of those who know nothing about the case are happy. But the questions are not answered.

A study of the two phenomena may answer some questions that have puzzled the human race from the moment it became self-aware and could ask questions that transcended those of basic survival. The near-death phenomenon might give us a clue about what happens at the moment of death; and reincarnation might give us a clue about what happens in the days and months after death. It might not be the big black void that some would force us to believe it is.

In the long run this inquiry will show us that no information is useless in and of itself. There are questions to be answered about both the NDE and reincarnation, and those answers may help us improve our lives. Certainly nothing will be learned that won't be of use later.

So the two phenomena are related. They are related through common experience, common knowledge and common corroboration. Both can be seen as "New Age" or as science, but we must not allow study to end because "such things just aren't true."

The next time you are confronted by such a statement, point out that a hundred years ago, people couldn't fly through the air, travel in space, or watch a sporting event live even though it was taking place thousands of miles away. What can't be today will become what is tomorrow. Today's science is magic to those of a hundred years ago, and the technology of a hundred years from today will make our ideas of magic—into reality.

Sixteen

And In Conclusion . . .

Although I had heard about the near-death phenomenon before beginning this work, I knew next to nothing about it. I came into this with only the vaguest idea of what it meant. I believed, as did many of the theologians and skeptics, that it was all part of the New Age movement. That meant it was based, not on good research, but on the ramblings of those who bought into channeling, hauntings, and other aspects of the New Age.

Turned out I was wrong.

The thing that amazed me first, was the level of research being done. These were not wide-eyed investigations conducted by those who would believe anything about anything, but research done by trained medical doctors. It was surprising to learn that the first real book about the near-death experience had not been written by a New Age proponent, but by a

medical doctor reporting his observations of
hundreds of patients.

There has been a wide range of legitimate
research done by those competent to do it. The
gathering of the data, and the subsequent reporting of it, in papers, articles, and books, has
been handled, for the most part, professionally.
There are a large number of articles in professional journals discussing various aspects of
near-death. Clearly, there is no debate that
near-death experiences are real. The questions
center on the interpretation of those experiences.

As mentioned elsewhere, there is solid debate about what the near-death experience
means. In the cold, harsh light of journalism,
as we move through the various journals and
interview the various professionals, one picture
seems to emerge. Journalists and professionals
provide solid theories about what they believe
are prosaic events. Nothing spiritual about
them, just a phenomenon that we don't understand completely because no one has investigated it fully.

Paul Kurtz, chairman of the Committee for
the Scientific Investigation of Claims of the
Paranormal, writes that profound personality
change, one of the characteristics of the near-
death experience, is not evidence of an afterlife. He is correct. It is not proof of anything

other than the fact that the person having the experience is profoundly affected by it.

Kurtz cautions against the acceptance of data that have not been properly gathered. Again he is correct. We must maintain high standards, for to do less is to weaken the overall proof. And, we must not be afraid of following the path of truth, regardless of that truth. Sometimes those conducting research have an agenda to follow and are not concerned with the truth. Science, as well as many other arenas of human endeavor, has been guilty of that. We will never learn the truth if we cloud the research with what we want to believe, as opposed to what is the truth.

We have learned, in the last few years, that human memory is not solid and reliable. We learn that many who have the best of intentions, unconsciously direct their patients, clients, and friends, into beliefs that are not true. Families have been destroyed as children claim to have been abused, the "repressed" memories surfacing years, and sometimes decades, after the events. Too often, those memories are the creation of suggestive questioning, rather than real events.

Which is not to say that repressed memories don't exist and that people don't "spontaneously" remember long-forgotten events. A recent murder was solved when the daughter of the criminal remembered, spontaneously, the killing of her childhood friend by her father.

All this means is that we must proceed with caution when dealing with memories, and the activities of the human mind. There are too many areas in which we know next to nothing. We don't understand how memory works, how reliable it is, and how deep it goes. Does hypnotic regression allow us to remember better, or allow suggestion by the therapist to take on the compulsion to please? Witnesses who have been regressed are now sometimes kept from testifying in court. Dozens of papers by psychologists have been written about both memory and hypnosis. To say we don't understand it completely is to understate the case.

But all of this doesn't change the awe that fills the voices of those who have experienced the near-death phenomenon. It does not change the impressions they had, or the profound way it has affected their lives.

Beginning this work, I knew that I would want to speak to those who had near-death experiences. If nothing else, it would give me a clue about what it was like. I had assumed that it would be difficult to find someone with the experience. I had considered advertising in a newspaper, sending letters to the editors of big city dailies, or trying to find support groups that were concerned with NDE. In today's environment, if two people share a common experience, they create a support group to talk about it.

Finding those who had had the experience was simple. The Gallup Poll claimed that eight million Americans, or about one in thirty, had had such an experience. Just by mentioning it to a small group, I could find someone who had had an NDE, or knew someone who claimed one. Finding these people turned out to be a simple task.

And getting them to talk about the experience was also a simple task. They are delighted to share the experience. They want others to know about the glory of what they have seen. Many of the interviews were filled with laughing because of the sheer joy of the experience.

No, these people have had some very horrible experiences. One man was "killed" in Vietnam. Another "died" in a traffic accident. Several of them lost their lives in the hospital. That part, and the recovery from the wounds, injuries, or operations, is not pleasant. But the events during the period of death have been described as wonderful, beautiful, and glorious.

And yes, each of them talked of a profound change in life. Tom Dolembo mentioned that he found himself taking more time away from his studies or his work just so that he could enjoy the beautiful summer afternoon. Each claimed that they realized each day was precious, to be enjoyed.

With one exception, each said that they no longer had a fear of death. The one exception is the reverend who already had a strong faith and belief in God and Jesus. Now he was more convinced, if that is possible. The others said they no longer feared death at all. Being dead was not the dark expanse of nonexistence that some were frightened of, but something in which the individual survived the process of dying to continue to grow and learn.

Interestingly, many of them feared dying, but not death. Dying is the process, the wasting away by cancer, the sudden pain of a fatal traffic accident, or any of hundreds of horrible alternatives. But once they had died, then being dead was a wonderful thing.

All this is interesting, in an abstract way. The majority of us will not have a near-death experience. We'll do it once, and not be able to report to others what we felt, saw or learned. All we can do is speak with those who have "seen the light" and try to determine something about the experience through what they tell us, as I tried to do by writing this book. There was no way that I could experience it myself. Any test designed to find the tunnel and the light could easily be fatal. That was the plot of the movie *Flatliners*. These were medical students who would "kill" one another in a hospital environment under experimental conditions. Then they would jerk the "victim" back to see what he—or in a few cases, she—saw.

The flaw in the theory is that not everyone who has been pronounced clinically dead by doctors, but been resuscitated, has returned to life with a story of a near-death experience. Sometimes they have merely been unconscious. They weren't aware that they had "died" and can do nothing to increase our knowledge of what near-death is, or of what happens on the other side.

So, all we can do is talk to those "lucky" few and try to understand what they are saying to us. Maybe there is something to learn from what they say. It is clear, at least to me, that I am hearing the truth as they know it from these people. I have no reason to suspect they were making it up as they went along.

The one thing the printed word does not convey is the enthusiasm with which these people reported their experiences. The happiness as they talked about their experiences is difficult to express. The utter joy with which they try to communicate is lost in the dryness of a printed report.

But I have heard these stories from the people who had them. It was a learning experience for me. It changed my outlook on the near-death phenomenon, and in fact, changed my outlook on death. Although I have yet to "see the light," I have heard the stories of those

who have—from their own lips—and I have no
doubt about the truthfulness of those stories.

I have noticed, as I progressed in the inter-
viewing for this book, that I had changed the
tone of the questions. Rather than dancing
around the topic, trying to find a diplomatic
way to bring up the topic, I found myself becoming more frank simply because I realized
that it wasn't a topic that they didn't want to
talk about it. It was something they wanted to
share with all who had any desire to listen.

Death has always been a somewhat taboo subject. Insurance salesmen are taught not to use
the word death. It is always that you are out of
the picture. We use code words like passed
away, or are no longer with us. But with those
who have had these experiences, the words
change. They are not afraid, or even reluctant,
to speak of their own deaths. Either that death
already experienced or that death which has
yet to happen.

I find myself sharing such an attitude. I
seem to have joined their ranks without realizing it. My attitudes and concerns about death
have vanished as well. If nothing else, the work
on this book has paid a dividend in that respect. I believe the stories told by the people
who spoke to me.

As I pointed out in the Introduction, I have
done no investigative work. I interviewed a
number of people, I read the various research

papers and documents, and I looked at the
various books and magazine articles. But I have
not attempted to corroborate the information
provided by the people I spoke to.

One of the reasons is that I'm not sure what
good it would do. I could find the doctors who
treated the various people, I could confirm
their critical illnesses or injuries, but that
proves nothing either way. Besides, I have listened to the stories, listened to the tones of the
voice and find that I believe what I am told. I
have no doubt that they are relating, as best
they can, something they have experienced.

Maybe someday we will learn the truth about
the near-death experience. Maybe we will learn
that the psychologists are right about the reasons for the near-death experience . . . or
maybe we will learn that they reveal a little
about what happens when we die.

Sometimes it seems that we want to know too
much. Sometimes we learn things that we are
better off not knowing. There are those who
believe the world would be better if the atomic
bomb had never been built. But that sort of
question is always open for debate.

As it stands now, we don't have the answers.
We don't know what those who experience
near-death are actually seeing. We don't know
how the mind operates in those conditions. All
we know, for certain, is that the phenomenon
is real. It is the interpretation that is in dispute.

But for me, and for those eight million others, near-death is a glimpse of what happens when we die. It provides a level of comfort and hope, and if nothing else, there isn't anything wrong with that.

Seventeen

How to Prepare for the Near-Death Experience

There is very little that can be done to prepare for the near-death experience. By its very definition, it is not planned. It is, instead, an outgrowth of circumstances that we are unable to control. We must be at the point of death, reaching that point by accident, illness, or tragic mistake.

Those searching for Bigfoot, UFOs, or Atlantis, can plan. They can carry cameras, film, video tape, recorders, maps, and many other instruments. They can create a record that can be taken into a laboratory to be studied. It might be nothing more than measurements made on photos, the study of negatives, or computer enhancement of video tape, but it is something that is open to study by others. Locations can be plotted and others can "stake out" those locations. If it is evidence of Atlantis, others can travel to that location for their own study. Independent verification of the data is possible.

But with near-death, almost the whole of the phenomenon relies on witness testimony. What records and readings available mark the reality of the situation of the body rather than what the mind is doing. Readings, often available because of the situation, can demonstrate that a body was clinically dead. Sometimes they show that the brain is dead with no electrical activity, or that the person is physically dead ready for autopsy and burial.

Those readings, however, prove absolutely nothing. The lack of electrical activity in the brain can be explained by suggesting the activity was so deep in the brain and at such a low level that it could not be detected by current instruments. It is possible that better instruments with finer capability to discriminate might have produced some results. Definitions of death are altered as it becomes clear that we understand little of what we thought we knew.

So, there is no way to prepare for a near-death experience, nor is there a way to gather data that would provide the sort of evidence that a scientifically trained mind would need. There is nothing to photograph and no way to prove that the visions were of the other side. Proof will eventually be found by all of us, but at that point it is too late. We will have already crossed over to the other side and will not be returning to explain what happened or what we saw.

However, there are some common-sense things to be done as soon as possible after the event. Timing is everything. If possible, the time in this world should be established. It will provide researchers with an anchor for the event.

The thoughts upon return, and the memories of the event should be recorded as quickly as possible. All feelings, emotions, impressions and descriptions should be written down or taped. According to some researchers, the first impressions, available in the moments just after resuscitation are significantly different from the impressions spoken of hours or days later. The first impressions, when possible, should be recorded.

If the incident takes place in a hospital, while the patient under treatment or on the operating table, the various records should be gathered at the time. As the "victim" of the near-death experience, these records should be available to you. Later, if there is controversy, then some form of documentation will be available.

Betty Malz, who claims two near-death experiences, does not have the proper documentation. Clearly, if she had the records, then one aspect of her story could be corroborated.

Without them, acceptance of her experience by others is more difficult. While it doesn't prove there was a NDE, or that the interpretation of the event is accurate, it does establish a certain level of corroboration.

If, during the experience, some sort of predictive information is provided, as some have suggested, then another level of corroboration is available. One woman said that she learned of several natural or man-made disasters which would happen in the near future. She claimed to have known about the LA riots months before they broke out. Of course, that is what she claims after the events. Anyone can predict a disaster after it happens.

Predictions could be of value. If such information is obtained, then a sworn statement could be made. With the data out in the public arena, with witnesses to it, no questions about the validity of the prediction could be asked.

There is an old magician's trick for predicting the future. A sealed envelope with the prediction is given to a third party. Then, after a major event the envelope is opened to see how accurate the prediction is. Of course, the magician making the prediction is the one who opens the envelope. Using slight of hand, he removes the paper that had been sealed in the envelope and replaces it with another that more closely resembles the alleged prediction. This simple trick demands only manual dexterity.

But if the prediction is legitimate, there is no reason to seal it in anything. A public prediction, documented in the newspaper prior to the event, made to witnesses, or written out in the form of a notarized statement to be filed in the local county court house so that it can be reviewed by disinterested third parties, has no problems with authenticity. It would provide the proper documentation that would go a long way to corroboration of the near-death experience. It would not prove that the person had crossed to the other side, but it would certainly prove that the person had access to information that is clearly inexplicable. It would suggest other, more important questions.

For this to work, however, the prediction cannot be made in secret. It must be loudly proclaimed from the moment it is received. For science, the problem with most claims of paranormal activity, is that they are done in secret and will not withstand scientific scrutiny. When those claiming extrasensory perceptions are tested in controlled circumstances, they are rarely able to duplicate their successes inside the laboratory. If they can't do it under laboratory conditions, then science is right in its skepticism.

So, those who are to have a near-death experience can't plan for it. There is no instrumentation that can be used to record the event for scientific review of what is happening on the other side. All that can be done is to review the testimony of the person to determine how honest that person is. The readings of instruments at the time of "death" can be checked, but that proves nothing of use.

If, however, the Native Americans are right, and their rituals allow them to experience near-death, then experiments could be designed. Information could be gathered as various subjects allowed themselves to be placed in the "near-death state." Such experiments could enhance our knowledge of what happens after the moment of death. Of course, we would have to gather the data with the assistance of the Native Americans and they don't seem to be inclined to provide that help. After all, it would seem that they would have to violate their cultural heritage to provide that help and there doesn't seem to be a good reason to expect it.

The best advice is to be open to the experience. Observe as much as possible, record it as soon as possible, and share the experience with others when possible. As for planning for it, that can't be done.

Part V:
Bibliography

Bibliography

ALLEN, T. G., translator. *The Book of the Dead.* Chicago: University of Chicago Press, 1974.

ASCHER, Barbara. "Above All, Love." *Redbook* (February 1992) 30.

ATWATER, P. M. H. *Coming Back to Life: The After-Effects of the Near-Death Experience.* New York: Ballantine Books, 1991.

AYER, A. J. "What I Saw When I Was Dead." *National Review* (October 14, 1988) 38-40.

BARBANELL, Maurice. *He Walks in Two Worlds.* New York: Caravelle Books, Inc., 1964.

BATES, Brian C. and STANLEY, Adrian. "The Epidemiology and Differential Diagnosis of Near-Death Experience." *American Journal of Orthopsychiatry* (October 1985).

BERNSTEIN, Morey. *The Search for Bridey Murphy.* New York: Lancer Books, 1965.

BLACKMORE, Susan J. "Near-death Experiences: In or Out of the Body?" *Skeptical Inquirer* (Fall 1991) 34.

BRENNAN, J. H. *Astral Doorways*. New York: Samuel Weiser Inc. 1971.

BRUNVAND, Jan Harold. *The Choking Doberman and Other "New" Urban Legends*. New York: W.W. Norton & Company, 1984.

CHENEY, S. *Men Who Have Walked with God*. New York: Alfred A. Knopf, 1968.

CHERRY, Chris. "Near Death Experience and the Problem of Evidence for Survival After Death. *Religious Studies* (September/December 1986) 397-406.

———. "Self, Near-Death and Death." *International Journal for Philosophy of Religion* (1984) 3-11.

CLAPP, Rodney. "Rumors of Heaven." *Christianity Today* (October 7, 1988) 16-21.

COHEN, Daniel. "Bill McGowan: To the Edge and Back." *Business Week* (March 4, 1991) 46.

CORDES, Helen. "Facing Death." *Utne Reader* (September/October 1991) 65.

COTT, Jonathan. "People are Talking About Heaven: Is There Life After Life." *Vogue* (May 1987) 312, 369-71.

DETHLEFSEN, Thorwald. *Voices from Other Lives*. New York: M. Evans and Co., 1977.

DONNELLY, Ignatius. *Atlantis: The Antediluvian World*. New York: Gramercy Publishing Company, 1949.

EADIE, Betty J. *Embraced by the Light*. Placerville, CA: Gold Leaf Press, 1992.

EBERT, Alan. "A Glimpse of Heaven." *Redbook* (July 1991) 88-90.

FARRELL, Jeanette. "The Last Picture Show." *American Health* (May 1991) 14.

FERRIS, Timothy. "A Cosmological Event." *New York Times Magazine* (December 15, 1991) 44-45.

FERRO, Robert and GRUMLEY, Michael. *Atlantis—The Autobiography of a Search*. New York: Bell Publishing Company, 1970.

FIORE, Edith. *You Have Been Here Before*. New York: Coward, McCann and Geoghegan, 1978.

FISHER, Joe with COMMINS, Peter. *Predictions*. Toronto: William Collins Sons, 1980.

FORD, Arthur. *The Life Beyond Death*. New York: Berkley Medallion Books, 1971.

GREYSON, Bruce. "Near Death and Antisuicidal Attitudes." *Omega*, no. 2 (92/93) 81-89.

———. "Near Death Experience and Personal Values." *American Journal of Psychiatry* (May 1983) 618-20.

———. "A Typology of Near Death Experience." *American Journal of Psychiatry* (August 1985) 967-69.

GREYSON, Bruce and BUSH, Nancy Evan.

"Distressing Near Death Experiences." *Psychiatry* (February 1992).

GUILEY, Rosemary Ellen. *Tales of Reincarnation*. New York: Pocket Books, 1989.

HARPUR, Tom. "Passage to Paradise." *McLean's* (April 20, 1992) 40-41.

HAYES, Evelyn R. and WATERS, Linda D. "Interdisciplinary Perceptions of the Near Death Experience: Implications for Professional Education and Practice." *Death Studies* (1987).

HEAD, Joseph and CRANSTON, S. L., eds., *Reincarnation: The Phoenix Fire Mystery*. New York: Crown Publishers, 1977.

HOLZER, Hans. *Born Again: The Truth About Reincarnation*. Garden City, New York: Doubleday & Company, Inc., 1970.

JACOBBI, Marianne. "Your Wife May Never Wake Up." *Good Housekeeping* (June 1990) 161.

JAROFF, Leon. "Lies of the Mind." *Time* (November 29, 1993) 52-59.

JEROME, Jim. "Heaven Can Wait." *People Weekly* (October 11, 1993) 81.

KELLEHEAR, Allan. "The Near Death Experience as Status Passage." *Science and Medicine* 1990.

KLINENBORG, Verllye. "At the Edge of Eternity." *Life* (March 1992) 64-68.

KURTZ, Paul. "Scientific Evidence Keeps Us in the Here and Now. "Beyond Self." *Psychology Today* (September 1988) 15.

LANGLEY, Noel. *Edgar Cayce on Reincarnation.* New York: Paperback Library, 1967.

MAITZ, Edward, and PEHALA, Ronald J. "Phenomenological Qualifications of an Out-of-the-Body Experience Associated With a Near Death Event." *Omega 22* (90/91) 199-214.

MARTIN, Joel and ROMANOWSKI, Patricia. *We Don't Die: George Anderson's Conversations with the Other Side.* New York: G. P. Putnam's Sons, 1988.

MAURO, James. "Bright Lights, Big Mystery." *Psychology Today* (July/August 1992) 55-57, 80-82.

McCLAIN Florence Wagner. *A Practical Guide to Past Life Regression.* St. Paul, MN: Llewellyn's Publications, 1991.

McCLENON, James. "Near Death Folklore in Medieval China and Japan: A Comparative Analysis." *Asian Folklore Studies* (1991) 319-42.

MacREADY, Robert. *The Reincarnation of Robert MacReady.* New York: Zebra, 1980.

MEEK, George W. *After We Die, What Then?* Columbus, OH: Ariel Press, 1987.

MILLER, DeWitt. *Reincarnation—The Whole Startling Story.* New York: Bantam Books, 1956.

MONTGOMERY, Ruth. *Here and Hereafter.* New York: Coward-McCann, Inc. 1968.

MOODY, Raymond. *Life After Life.* New York: Bantam Books, 1976.

———. *The Light Beyond.* New York: Bantam Books, 1988.

MORSE, Melvin. "Children of the Light." *Reader's Digest* (March 1991) 83-86.

———. *Closer to the Light.* New York: Villard Books, 1990.

"My Brush with Death." *Ebony* (May 1989) 96.

NOLEER, Kathleen D. "Psychological Health and the Experience of Transcendence." *The Counseling Psychologist* (October 1987) 601-14.

O'BRIEN, Pamela Guthie. "Is There Life After Death?" *Lady's Home Journal* (September 1992) 158-60.

ORIEDGER, Sharon Doyle. "The Music in the Light." *McLean's* (April 20, 1992) 39.

OSIS, Karlis and HARALDSSON, Erlendur. *At the Hour of Death.* New York: Avon, 1977.

PEAY, P. "Back From the Grave." *Utne Reader* (September/October 1991) 72-73.

PERRY, Paul. "Brushes with Death." *Psychology Today* (September 1988) 14, 17.

PIZER, Vernon. "To Beyond and Back." *American Legion* (August 1991) 24.

RAUDIVE; Konstantin. *Is There Life After Life?*
New York: Zebra Books, 1971.

SCHORER; C. E. "Two Native American Near
Death Experiences." *Omega* (85/86) 111-13.

SERDAHELY, William. "The Near Death Experience: Is the Presence Always the Higher
Self? *Omega* 18 no. 2 (87/88) 129-34.

———. "A Pediatric Near-Death Experience:
Tunnel Variants." *Omega* (89/90) 55-62.

SHELTON, Kenya. "Second Wind." *Essence*
(May 1992) 48.

SIDEY, Ken. "Doctors Dispute Best-selling
Author's Back-to-Life Story." *Christianity Today*
(July 22, 1991) 41-43

SMITH, Susy. *Life is Forever.* New York: G. P.
Putnam's Sons 1974.

———. *The Enigma of Out-of-Body Travel.* New
York: Signet Mystic Books, 1968.

SPRAGGETT, Allen. *The Case for Immortality.*
New York: New American Library. 1974.

STEVENS, Carol. "I Felt Like I Was Going
Home." *Washingtonian* (September 1991) 82.

STEVENSON, Ian. *Cases of the Reincarnation
Type* (Vols. 1-4) Charlottesville: University Press
of Virginia, 1975-1983.

STEVENSON, Ian. COOK, Emily Williams,
McCLEAN, Rice. "Are Persons Reporting

'near death experiences' Really Near Death."
Omega (Farmingdale, NY) 89/90 20 no. 1 45-
54.

ST. JOHNS, Adela Rogers. *No Good-byes*. New
York: McGraw-Hill Book Company, 1981.

SUMMER, Bob. "Near-death Success." *Publisher's Weekly* (August 16, 1993) 31.

SUNSHINE-GENOVA, A. "The Near-death
Experience." *McCall's* (February 1988) 103-106.

TWEMLOW, Stuart W. and GABBARD, Glen
O. "The Influence of Demographic/Psycho-
logical Factors and Pre-existing Conditions on
the Near-Death Experience." *Omega* 15 no. 3
84/85 223-35.

UNDERWOOD, Nora. "Between Life and
Death." (April 20, 1992) 34-37.

———. "Glimpses of an Afterlife?" *McLean's*
(April 20, 1992) 38.

WALKER, Barbara. "Health Care Professionals
and the Near Death Experience. *Death Studies*
13 (1989).

WATERS, Craig. *The Quest for Eternity*.
Rockville Centre, NewYork: Playboy Paper-
backs, 1982.

WHITTON, Joel L. and FISHER, Joe. *Life Between Life*. Garden City, NY: Doubleday & Co.
Inc., 1986.